W9-AEJ-873

What We Know About:

Culture and Learning

EDUCATIONAL RESEARCH SERVICE

Because research and information make the difference.

Educational Research Service
2000 Clarendon Boulevard, Arlington, VA 22201-2908
Tel: (703) 243-2100 or (800) 791-9308
Fax: (703) 243-1985 or (800) 791-9309
Email: ers@ers.org • Web site: www.ers.org

Educational Research Service is the nonprofit foundation serving the research and information needs of the nation's K-12 education leaders and the public. Founded by seven national school management associations, ERS provides quality, objective research and information that enables local school district administrators to make the most effective school decisions, both in terms of day-to-day operations and long-range planning. Refer to the last page of this publication to learn how you can benefit from the services and resources available through an annual ERS Subscription.

ERS offers a number of research-based resources that particularly complement this report on early reading instruction. Please refer to the Order Form on page 91 of this publication for a listing of some of these materials. Alternatively, visit us online at www.ers.org for a more complete overview of the wealth of K-12 research and information products and services available through ERS.

ERS Founding Organizations:
American Association of School Administrators
American Association of School Personnel Administrators
Association of School Business Officials International
Council of Chief State School Officers
National Association of Elementary School Principals
National Association of Secondary School Principals
National School Public Relations Association

Ordering information: Additional copies of *What We Know About: Culture and Learning* may be purchased at the base price of $20.00 each (ERS Comprehensive subscriber price: $9.00; ERS Individual subscriber price: $13.50). Quantity discounts available. Stock No. 0491. ISBN 1-931762-10-4.

Order from: ERS Member Services Information Center, Educational Research Service, 2000 Clarendon Boulevard, Arlington, VA 22201-2908. Telephone: (800) 791-9308. Fax: (800) 791-9309. Email: msic@ers.org. Web site: www.ers.org. Add the greater of $3.50 or 10% of total purchase price for postage and handling. Phone orders accepted with Visa, MasterCard, or American Express.

ERS Management Staff:
John M. Forsyth, Ph.D., President
Joseph J. D'Amico, Vice President
Katherine A. Behrens, Senior Director of Marketing and Member Services
Patrick R. Murphy, Senior Director of Finance and Administration

Note: The views expressed in *What We Know About: Culture and Learning* are those of the authors and do not necessarily reflect the official positions of Educational Research Service or its founding organizations.

Table of Contents

Authors: Leona M. Johnson with the assistance of Nancy Protheroe.

Leona M. Johnson is a doctoral student in Educational Psychology at Howard University in
Washington, D.C., and is currently completing dissertation research on the topic of "Learning
Preferences of Students in Mid-Atlantic, Metropolitan, Elementary, Schools." Other related work
includes a presentation on "Teaching Styles and Learning Preferences" at a Learning and Cognition
Symposium presentation on "Teaching Styles and Learning Preferences" at Howard University.

Nancy Protheroe is Director of Special Research Projects at Educational Research Service. She is
responsible for coordinating research and writing projects such as the *What We Know About* series and
has written on topics such as effective instruction, special education, and the characteristics of
successful schools and districts.

Foreword

This publication, *What We Know About: Culture and Learning,* is part of the Educational Research Service's continuing effort to provide comprehensive resources about areas of interest to education leaders. The *What We Know About* series is designed to present in a brief and understandable way what is currently known about specific practices and issues of special need to educators who are working to help all students achieve at high levels. Each publication provides readers with a balanced discussion of the practical research, relevant information, and informed opinion contained in the professional literature on the subject.

This report highlights reasons why attention to culture and learning is of ever-increasing importance to our schools. It examines the relationship between culture and learning, and discusses how conflicts between the culture of their homes and that of typical classrooms can hinder the educational process for many students. It reviews examples of culturally sensitive instructional practices, and describes the considerations that teachers and school administrators need to take into account as they attempt to meet the needs of a student population that is growing more culturally diverse.

Concentrating on how students learn and how teachers teach, *What We Know About: Culture and Learning* describes instructional techniques that incorporate cultural awareness, maintain standards of excellence, avoid racial stereotypes, and foster high expectations for students of all ethnic backgrounds in today's schools and classrooms.

As with all the publications in the *What We Know About* series, the focus is on building from what we already know about effective practice and then using this research to help close the achievement gap. As educators work to address problems of low achievement by often substantial portions of their student populations, a better understanding of how culture can affect learning provides another tool to help teachers reach and teach their students and improve student achievement.

John M. Forsyth
President

Introduction

Cultural diversity is the well-established norm for many schools and school districts today, and few teachers can assume a homogeneity of student cultures, languages, and background experiences in their classrooms. In his overview of 10 trends that will have a profound impact on society and on schools in the United States, Gary Marx amply demonstrates that attention to culture will become even more important during the first half of this new century. Using data from the Population Division of the U.S. Bureau of the Census, he contends:

> By mid-century, no single group will make up a significant majority of the U.S. population. Shortly after 2050, the United States will become a nation of minorities… The projections are revealing…. By 2050, the longstanding non-Hispanic White majority will represent 53 percent of the population, down from 71 percent in 2000…. An even smaller proportion of youth (birth to age 18) will be White—46 percent in 2050, compared to 64 percent in 2000 (2000, 6).

In Holmes' 2001 view, our nation is not only rapidly becoming more diverse, the diversity is more complex. For example, it is important that educators understand that students who have moved here from Southeast Asia may have vastly different attitudes toward, and experiences with, schooling depending on the country—or region within a country—from which they have emigrated. Our understanding of culture has also broadened. We now understand that being aware of cultural differences means more than attending to the needs of students who have recently moved to this country.

Culture and the Achievement Gap

Trumbell, Rothstein-Fisch, and Greenfield address the broader implications of culture for schools:

>It's not only immigrant students whose cultural values may differ from those underlying most classroom practice. U.S.-born students from a variety of backgrounds—American Indian, African American students, Latino students whose families have lived here for generations—may also feel alienated by common classroom practices (2000, online).

Steinberg, Brown, and Dornbusch elaborate on the need to view the problems of culture as more broadly based than simply dealing with immigrant students or those who have limited English proficiency:

>…the differences between ethnic groups are not simply due to ethnic differences in income or parental education. That is, Asian students from low-income homes outperform comparably disadvantaged White, Black, and Latino students, and low-income White students score higher that comparably disadvantaged Black or Latino students; middle-class Asian students outperform middle-class Whites, who, in turn, outperform middle-class Black and Latino students; and so on…. Nor can the differences be attributable to differences in the schools youngsters attend, since we find these ethnic differences even among youngsters enrolled in the same schools (1996, 31).

To address this problem, research has focused on the question of the role that culture might play in the achievement gap between Black and Latino and non-Latino White students and characterized by some as one of the most pressing problems in education (Viadero, 2000). Since the 1960s, researchers have documented how African American children lag behind White youngsters in their performance on standardized tests. Although the gap appeared to be narrowing throughout the 1980s, tests such as the National Assessment of Educational Progress (NAEP) indicate that the progress made is now being eroded (Hoff 2000). Michael Nettles, vice chairman of the National Assessment Governing Board, characterizes this as "a depressing reversal of the gains that were made over the previous two decades" (Hoff 2000).

After reviewing extensive data about student achievement, the National Task Force Report on Minority High Achievement found that the gaps are evident in early elementary school and persist throughout schooling (Viadero 1999). While some portion of the gap may be related to higher rates of poverty among Black students, Townsend makes it clear that this is not the only reason:

[The] gap is not entirely explainable by poverty and other factors. For example, recent studies show that the achievement gap is actually wider between African American middle class students and their European American middle class peers than it is between African Americans from low income backgrounds and their European American counterparts with similar family income levels (2000, 5).

One of these studies was done in Shaker Heights, Ohio, an affluent suburb of Cleveland.

While Blacks constituted more than half of the school enrollment, they accounted for fewer than 10 percent of the top-achieving students and 90 percent of those at the bottom (Viadero and Johnston 2000; *Newsweek* 1999).

School efforts to close the gap in academic achievement between ethnic and racial minority students and White students have been largely unsuccessful to date; differences in educational performance persist at all achievement levels, with the gap greatest between students of color and immigrants and their White and Asian American peers at high achievement levels. The need for a solution to this problem has new urgency now—here in the increasingly diverse United States—as the relationship between educational success and social and economic opportunity steadily strengthens and the relationship between educational differences and social conflict becomes more manifest (Schwartz 2001, online).

Although there has been no research that definitively identifies the reasons for this gap, what is certain is that a complex combination of school, community, and home factors is at work. The possibility of a misalignment between the culture of many classrooms and the home culture of many students of color is just one of these factors, but one that schools can address without sacrificing standards.

What Can Schools Do?

All of this means that ever-increasing demands are being placed on schools and on education professionals. Add to this the push for higher standards, such as those mandated in the recent federal No Child Left Behind legislation, and the need for schools to focus classroom instruction on the needs of individual students becomes ever more apparent.

This is happening at a time when teachers of color make up only about 10 percent of the work force in public schools, with even that small percentage diminishing (Landsman 2001). The contrast between the demographics of the student population and teachers underscores the critical role that *all* teachers must play in learning about and being responsive to cultural differences in society (Hollins and Oliver 1999).

Faced with the challenge discussed above, many educators today are asking difficult questions about cultural diversity and schooling. What cultural differences are present in schools? How do these differences influence the teaching and learning process? How can schools best ensure instructional excellence and equity for all students in a heterogeneous environment?

This publication addresses some of these questions by reviewing the professional literature on cultural differences and their impact on learning processes and effective teaching. Current research suggests that culture strongly influences students' learning patterns, communication styles, perceptions, and behavior. The research profiled here details ways that teachers can improve student learning by becoming aware of such cultural differences and employing "culturally sensitive" instructional methods.

The term "culture" as it is used in this book refers to ways of being, knowing, and doing.

Culturally sensitive instruction seeks an educationally productive balance between commonality and diversity in heterogeneous schools and classrooms. Commonality is emphasized through the universal acquisition of a common set of basic skills necessary to function in school and in mainstream society. The cultural diversity present in the classroom is also recognized, respected, and used as an instructional resource. In culturally sensitive instruction, teachers regard the academic success of *all* students as fundamental. They seek to incorporate appropriate instructional strategies and create learning environments that most effectively motivate and teach each student to succeed.

The term "culture" as it is used in this book refers to ways of being, knowing, and doing. Originally from the field of anthropology, this type of usage is often found in research that examines the impact of culture on cognition, communication, motivation, language development, and behavior. Information gained from such research can be applied to help teachers better understand student learning processes and classroom interactions. Culture as it is used here does not address *what* students learn because it is assumed that high standards are applied to all students. Instead, it examines *how* students learn, regardless of the subject area or content being taught.

Chapter One:
Why Culture Matters

It has long been recognized that cultural variables influence how children present themselves, understand the world, and interpret experiences. Culture also affects the experiences through which children's earliest literacy and mathematical knowledge are acquired. Some of these experiences may be explicitly focused on encouraging learning, such as reading books to children or instructing them in how to count. More common are the activities that provide implicit, unintentional support for various types of learning in the context of shared everyday activities. Significant as well are the adult activities that children witness and interpret as enjoyable or useful because their parents and relatives engage in them ("Cultural Diversity and Early Education: Report of a Workshop" 1994).

Early Learning Experiences

Research on culture and learning begins with the assumption that children are not "empty vessels" when they enter the educational system. They have already internalized standards of communication, interaction, language use, and behavior from their home environments (Saville-Troike 1978). Cultural traditions and values all heavily influence parenting styles, family structures, and rules for social interaction. These cultural modes help to determine the shape of childrens' earliest learning experiences.

This process is illustrated by the influence of Native American cultural patterns on children's learning experiences. Young children in some Native American cultures are regularly encouraged to be spectators at many adult activities such as community meetings or the parents' workday. Children in these situations learn about their environments through observation and imitation, rather than through direct verbal instruction. In this context, children become skilled observers of the nonverbal and behavioral cues of the adults around them. Research suggests that Native American students who have these early experiences develop visual-spatial learning styles and use nonverbal communication strategies more frequently than verbal ones. These cultural patterns contrast sharply with European American patterns that tend to segregate adult/child activities and often rely heavily on verbal modes of instruction and expression (Henry and Pepper 1990).

The literature regarding culturally sensitive instruction normally emphasizes possible teaching/learning differences among racial/ethnic groups. However, when culture is defined as "ways of being, knowing, and doing," variations in socioeconomic class or community type can also present real possibilities for cultural conflict. For example, a classic study conducted by Heath (1982) found that the parent-child interactions differed between the middle- and lower-class children she studied. Specifically, middle-class parents were more likely to talk with their children about the books they read to them at bedtime and to ask "why" questions, while reading for the lower-class children consisted of focusing on letters and names of objects. The experiences of these children left them less well prepared for the culture of most classrooms.

Culture does *not* determine a child's ability or intelligence. But it can produce many different ways of knowing and learning.

Both of these examples demonstrate that a child's cultural context can influence how he or she processes and organizes information, communicates verbally and nonverbally, and perceives physical and social environments. Each of these factors in turn can shape a child's learning patterns and affect later school experiences. Culture does *not* determine a child's ability or intelligence. But it can produce many different ways of knowing and learning.

Cultural Discontinuity

Mainstream schools are often structured to reflect and operate according to middle-class European American cultural standards. Students from different cultural backgrounds can experience culture conflicts in such classrooms because their accustomed ways of learning and communicating may not match mainstream routines.

Trumbell, Rothstein-Fisch, and Greenfield remind us of how interwoven culture is in our daily lives—and in the daily lives of schools:

> Culture is like the air we breathe, permeating all we do. And the hardest culture to examine is often our own, because it shapes our actions in ways that seem second nature.... Like individuals and groups, schools have cultures, too. These usually mirror the culture of the dominant society. We know the struggle many children and their parents face in learning English as a second language, and we understand that refugees from troubled homelands often bring emotional burdens. But we may not realize what an enormously difficult transition many must make in learning to decipher a new culture. This is often true, too, for native-born American children when the cultural values at home differ significantly from those of school (2000, online).

They also discuss the role of the teacher in identifying, interpreting, and addressing the needs of particular "cultural ways of knowing and behaving":

> Teachers who serve each day as cultural mediators know the challenge goes beyond language. Even as they try to help immigrant students navigate a new system of education, their own teaching methods and most routine classroom expectations can come into perplexing conflict with children's cultural ways of knowing and behaving. For example, a student may resist offering the right answer after another student has answered incorrectly, in order not to embarrass that person in front of the group. A student raised to value consensus may find decisions made by majority rule inconsiderate or even unfair, instead of simply democratic.... Teachers in these diverse school settings quickly discover the need for social understanding that goes beyond the relatively superficial aspects of culture often addressed in multicultural education, such as major holidays, religious customs, dress and foods. What's missing, teachers report, is a deeper kind of understanding—of the social ideals, values, and behavioral standards that shape approaches to child-rearing and schooling, first in one's own culture and then in the cultures of one's students (2000, online).

Culture and Learning

Culture conflicts can interfere with a child's progress by producing misunderstanding, discomfort, possible rejection, and, ultimately, low achievement. Jordan summarizes this process of conflict:

> By the time children come to school, they have already learned very complex material as part of being socialized into their own culture. This means that in minority schooling we are dealing with a situation involving two cultures—the culture of the school and the culture of the child. When the two are not compatible, the school fails to teach and the child fails to learn (1984, 61).

This theory, often called the *cultural discontinuity* approach, suggests that *culture conflict,* rather than low ability or the lack of desire to succeed, is often the reason that the achievement of children from some ethnic groups lags behind that of their majority-group peers. Nelson-Barber describes this conflict as "transactional"—something that happens *between* the school and the student and not something inherent to the student (1999, 11).

When different social systems interact, the normative rules of procedure often conflict. Many of the instructional procedures used by schools stem from a set of cultural values, orientations, and perceptions that differ radically from those of many of our students. Research findings suggest that contexts for learning and performance that are more responsive to the child's familiar and prevailing cultural experiences may facilitate the child's cognitive functioning, and consequently his or her achievement (Boykin and Bailey 2000). Educational practice will be improved when educators identify mismatches between the culture that children bring to school and the culture of the school (Hale 1994). Synergism between home and school culture can only strengthen the cultural and intellectual capital of all students, including minority students.

Koki reminds us that our growing knowledge about how children learn provides a helpful context in which to place a discussion of the role that culture—the culture of the home and the culture of the school—plays in education:

> Education research has made major breakthroughs in understanding how children learn. We now know that how well children learn often depends on how well they relate new information or knowledge to their daily lives and experiences. This constructivist philosophy has heightened educators' interest in how learning is influenced by children's cultural

experiences. And it has led to a re-examination of teaching strategies used in traditional cultures that have significant implications for educators everywhere. Traditional academic curricula have not reflected the learning cultures from which many students come. As a result, many have failed or have not been as successful in school as they might have been.

At one time in the United States, students could still do well in life even if they were not good at "book learning." Unfortunately, given the socioeconomic and demographic changes in the nation, this is no longer the case. In general, children who do not do well in school also do not succeed outside of school. Students' prospects for success are improved by implementing strategies that draw on their strengths and past knowledge and experiences, rather than on their economic and academic inadequacies. The challenge is to teach the academic curriculum we expect all children to complete using problems and situations that carry meaning from students' own experiences. The findings from research are transforming the methods that are being used to teach Western subjects to students in traditional societies—a group that commonly experiences high rates of school failure in Hawaii and the Pacific entities. Educators are also recognizing that many of the same principles being successfully used with minority children also apply to teaching non-Native Americans (Koki n.d., 1).

While advocates of culturally sensitive instruction accept that culture conflicts cannot be held wholly responsible for low achievement among some cultural and racial groups, they are also firm in their belief that addressing them can make a positive difference. Combined with high expectations for students, an awareness of cultural differences and the implementation of even small-scale changes in instructional practices can improve teacher-student communication and help to create supportive environments that maximize student achievement.

It must also be emphasized here that culture conflicts are more often the products of misunderstanding or lack of awareness than products of antipathy or racism. "No teacher goes to school in the morning with the desire to hurt a child [but] our practices, not by design but in effect, allow success to be attained only by some" (Sher and Weast 1991, 9-10). The task at hand for teachers is to improve success for all students by gaining an awareness of and sensitivity to the effects of culture and cultural differences.

While advocates of culturally sensitive instruction accept that culture conflicts cannot be held wholly responsible for low achievement among some cultural and racial groups, they are also firm in their belief that addressing them can make a positive difference.

Learning to interpret across cultures demands reflecting on our own experiences, analyzing our own culture, and examining and comparing varying perspectives. We must consciously and voluntarily make our cultural lenses apparent. Engaging in the hard work of seeing the world as others see it must be a fundamental goal of any effort to address cultural conflicts in the classroom (Delpit 1995).

Some Problematic Results of Culture Conflicts in Schooling

When students are labeled by terms such as "disadvantaged," "at-risk," "bilingual," or "minority," they are frequently perceived as deficient in some way (Villegas 1991, 9). Cultural differences increase the possibility that this perception of deficiency can occur, because some behaviors of these students can be misinterpreted as indications of either a lack of learning ability or a lack of interest in learning.

As an example of a potential problem area, Bowers and Flinders point out that "a student's silence [in response to a teacher's question] could mean that the student simply does not know the answer . . . or it may reflect a cultural pattern that prescribes how children should relate to adults" (1991, 7). Here, the teacher and child have different views of appropriate behavior: the teacher expects an immediate response, but the child has been taught to show respect by waiting a short period before answering. If this incongruity happens often enough, the teacher might wrongly judge the child as not learning because of inability or lack of interest.

Thus, misinterpretation of cultural differences as indications of low academic ability can result in instructional practices and subtle teacher behaviors that communicate to students that less learning is expected of them—and therefore can reduce their academic achievement.

The following section briefly discusses some aspects of schooling that affect all students but have special significance when culture conflict is added to the equation. For example, in regard to the potentially harmful effects of ability grouping on students whose cultures do not match those of the mainstream classroom and so are more likely to be placed in with other students who are considered low-achieving, Villegas concludes that,

> . . . rather than narrowing the gap between the groups, the instructional practices used with the less-advanced students tend to accentuate any inequality in skills and knowledge that may be present when children are initially admitted to school. For this reason, the over-representation of minority children in low-level tracks gives cause for alarm (1991, 9).

Recent reports have focused specifically on the high incidence of Black students classified as eligible for special education services and the comparatively low numbers of Black students who are enrolled in Advanced Placement courses (Patton 1998).

Since culture may act to limit teachers' expectations for students if the ways in which students interact with instruction and assessment do not correspond to a teacher definition of a "competent" student, this discontinuity can have a troubling and potentially damaging effect on student learning. For over two decades, educational researchers have been concerned with the possibility that teachers communicate different performance expectations for students they believe to have low versus high achievement potential. In planning for and interacting with entire classes, small groups, and individuals, teachers are guided by their beliefs about how students will respond if treated in particular ways. For example, Good (1987) found that teachers often demanded less work from students they viewed as "slow," gave them accurate feedback less often, and waited a shorter time for them to answer questions.

Research has also shown that teachers' expectations for students tend to be self-fulfilling. That is, students tend to give to teachers as much or as little as teachers expect of them (Lumsden 1997). And from their first years in school, students are able to perceive differences in teachers' expectations for their own performance and that of their peers (Gottfredson et al. 1995). On a more positive note, when teachers and administrators maintain high expectations, they encourage in students a desire to aim high rather than slide by (Lumsden 1997). A number of studies have also found a positive relationship between the teacher's sense of efficacy and students' classroom achievement.

One reason appears to be that teachers with a low sense of efficacy place responsibility for learning almost solely on the students. Taken as a whole, the research literature on teacher efficacy shows that teachers who believe they can make a difference do make a difference. In contrast, those who believe they cannot be successful act in ways that ensure that prophecy will come true. Low self-efficacy teachers fail both their students and themselves. But given appropriate support, encouragement, and development, these teachers, too, begin to view themselves as more efficacious and effective (Weber and Omotani 1994).

Understanding Sources of Culture Conflict in the Classroom

Every classroom is a community in which the pattern of interactions between teacher and students creates a culture. Villegas (1991) describes the organizational and cultural features of the typical classroom as follows: the teacher selects the topics of discussion and allocates turns to talk; learning is equated with talking, and silence is therefore interpreted as lack of learning; one person is allowed to speak at a time; individual competition is favored over group cooperation; and topics are introduced in small, sequenced steps. Some children are well prepared by their home backgrounds to function in this typical classroom culture; for them, the school experience is a comfortable extension of the home experience. For many children, however, the culture of the classroom clashes with their home and community background.

Koki explains the notion of the impact of cultural differences on education in common sense terms:

> Past experiences are key determinants of how students interpret concepts and events in the classroom. Perhaps one of the most important findings about learning is that comprehension is not transferred directly from a source—the teacher—to a learner. Instead, the brain "filters" information to make sense of it in light of what the learner already knows. In today's diverse classrooms, students have many experiences and knowledge bases that may not be familiar to teachers from the "mainstream" culture. Researchers suspect that many teachers—whether they are dealing with minority children who are geographically isolated or inner city children in a highly urban setting—may inadvertently overlook what children already know, and thus fail to connect the informa-

tion or skills the children need to have with the children's prior experiences (Koki n.d., 2).

Cultural conflicts or discontinuities can take many different forms, some of which hold the potential to adversely affect teacher-student relationships, the learning process, and student outcomes. The ultimate goal of the study of culture conflict is not to create a list of cultural features that "explain" students' school behaviors. Rather, researchers seek information that can help teachers understand the wide spectrum of group and individual variations that are present within their classrooms and the complex and interconnected ways these variations can affect student learning.

Saravia-Shore and Garcia talk about why understanding the classroom as the dominant culture is important:

> When the norms of interaction and communication in a classroom are very different from those to which the student has been accustomed, students experience confusion and anxiety, cannot attend to learning, and may not know how to appropriately seek the teacher's attention, get the floor, or participate in discussion. (Saravia-Shore and Garcia 1995, 57).

Ziegahn reminds us that instructional strategies are "not neutral." For example, activities such as "an individual learner's presentation of a project in front of the class or leadership in large-group discussion . . . is valued in a culture that promotes individual assertion and initiative [but] . . . may be perplexing for a learner coming from a culture where the question of who speaks from a position of leadership or power is highly dependent upon age, gender, or status as a student" (2001, online).

Finally, Graybill stresses the obligation of teachers to view and work with student differences as assets, not liabilities:

> In this age of diversity, we educators must surely recognize that it is no longer acceptable to use one method of teaching all students.... Teachers must avoid measuring black children against a white norm, which leads to thinking in terms of deficit education and compensatory skills rather than focusing on how best to accommodate African American learning styles. Differences in learning should be considered just that— differences in learning, not differences in ability (1997, 314).

From a pragmatic perspective, teachers may not be able to anticipate all culture conflicts or have knowledge of every cultural subtlety displayed by each student in a heterogeneous and constantly changing school environment. However, it is vital that teachers be familiar with the following basic themes and principles contained in the literature on culture, learning, and intercultural interaction:

♦ Culture affects learning patterns through its influence on cognition, language use, motivation, attitudes, and communication.

♦ Effective communication is an absolute requirement for effective teaching. "Language (and more broadly communication) is more than just the content of spoken messages; it includes changes in voice pitch, rhythm, and the use of the body and social space as additional sources of information" (Bowers and Flinders 1991, 6).

♦ While some feelings, experiences, and knowledge areas are universal, ways of expressing and processing them vary widely from culture to culture (Varney and Cushner 1990, 91). Patterns of expression and interaction taken for granted within the dominant culture are not always universally shared (Bowers and Flinders 1991, 22).

♦ The cultural forces affecting learning and communication may be beyond our control or immediate personal experience. They are not, however, beyond our understanding or awareness (Abi-Nader 1991, 549).

These principles—and the "Key Areas of Cultural Difference" shown in the box on page 17—provide lenses through which teachers working in culturally diverse classrooms can consciously examine the behaviors of students and of themselves.

Cultural Characteristics that Can Impact the Teacher-Learner Connection

Included in this section is information about some of the aspects of culture that can create disconnects between the teacher and the learner. Embedded in the discussion—and in some resources about several cultures—are descriptions of how specific cultures view the world, interact with other people, etc.

Key Areas of Cultural Difference

Cultures tend to vary along a number of dimensions. The following are among those in which different views and behaviors can lead to misunderstanding and tension:

◆ *Individualism and Collectivism.* Individualistic cultures generally value the self-reliance, equality, and autonomy of the individual, whereas collectivist cultures tend to value group effort and harmony and knowing one's place within society. For example, mainstream U.S. workplace cultures are often fragmented over the balance between rewarding individual effort and competition versus recognizing and fostering teamwork and cooperation.

◆ *Monochronic and Polychronic Time.* "M-time" is tangible and can be "saved, spent, wasted, lost, made up . . . and run out." Personal interaction can be sacrificed to scheduling and efficiency. "P-time," however, stresses involvement of people and completion of transactions rather than preset schedules.

◆ *Egalitarianism versus Hierarchy.* Believing in fairness and equal opportunities for everyone is critical in more individualistic cultures that often equate hierarchy with rigidity, even if equality is more of a societal ideal than a reality. Conversely, hierarchy may be valued in more collectivist cultures as a means of acknowledging innate differences and inequalities and of facilitating communication through the recognition of various social levels through titles and roles.

◆ *Action versus "Being" Orientation.* U.S. culture generally tends to value action, efficiency, getting to "the bottom line," often downplaying social interactions in the interest of achieving goals. Taking time to discuss and understand complex issues and to appreciate the moment may be more important to people coming from a more holistic cultural orientation than the perception of precipitously moving to action steps.

◆ *Change and Tradition.* "Change" has become the mantra of dominant U.S. society, which looks toward the future and resists an historical perspective. Those coming from cultures that value the lessons of history view the past as an important guide to the present and the future.

◆ *Communication Styles.* How we communicate is often as important as what we communicate. Depending partially on cultural variables such as nationality, ethnicity, gender, and race (among others), individuals may have a reference for both sending and receiving messages in styles that are linear or circular, direct or indirect, attached or detached, procedural or personal, and more confrontational in either intellectual or relational terms.

◆ *Power Imbalances.* In addition to the differences in values and communication styles that contribute to cultural diversity, cultures are stratified by inequities in terms of access to political and economic power. Thus, a culture's relative advantage or disadvantage depends on its position vis-à-vis other cultural groups (Ziegahn 2001, online).

A Caution against Stereotyping

While information about cultural characteristics can be helpful to teachers, a caution is also in order. These descriptions can only provide some possibilities to consider. They should *not* be used to create a picture of one specific child. For instance, to assume without inquiry that Therese as an immigrant from a Central American country will prefer cooperative to individual work may do a disservice both to Therese and to a system of instruction that is based on identified needs rather than common stereotypes.

It is important for educators to keep in mind that, within any given ethnic group, individuals vary greatly in their experiences, beliefs, and practices. All children, regardless of their heritage, will display individual preferences and variations in personality, learning patterns, and behavior. While general cultural information can give us useful and important clues about learners, it is still essential for teachers to regard every student as an individual.

> Even within highly individualistic or collectivistic cultures, people are, of course, treated both as individuals and as members of a group. It's the relative emphasis that makes for important differences and, sometimes, for conflicts. Similarly, people from the same general cultural background may nonetheless show wide variations in behavior, based on their level of formal schooling and socioeconomic status, among other things. More schooling and higher socioeconomic status are generally associated with greater individualism. Poor immigrants from rural sectors of very collectivistic cultures are therefore likely to encounter the most conflict in schools… The experiences of the Bridging Cultures teachers show that awareness of the causes of such conflicts almost always leads to new thinking about solutions. Some solutions are quite simple and easily carried out (Trumbell, Rothstein-Fisch, and Greenfield 2000, online).

Some of the methods that can be used to avoid stereotyping of students include observation of students' school behaviors, the use of parent interviews or home-school connections, and the administration of learning style inventories. Community members are also a good source of information and can act as liaisons between parents and the school. Such information-gathering techniques can help provide teachers with the necessary data to make more accurate and unbiased decisions about appropriate instruction for each student.

Another aspect of stereotypes relates to the tendency to think of the problems of cultural conflicts as though they are limited to foreign-born children or children from certain ethnic or racial groups. Addressing only the needs of these children will ignore the differences in life experiences between, for example, middle-class and poor White children. Often, these children vary by more than just the academic or prereading skills they bring to school. Variations include adult/child interaction patterns, the behaviors considered appropriate for children, and the expectations of the family with regard to home-school relationships. These are all part of the child's culture, and for some children that culture may be one that does not mesh easily with the general culture of the school.

"Time" as a Cultural Variable

Sileo and Prather remind us that even a concept as seemingly simple as "time" can be a source of cultural conflict since, in contrast to the culture in most U.S. classrooms that is quite structured from the perspective of time, students from some cultures focus on the task and see time as much less important. In the view of these authors,

> Teachers who lack sensitivity to this cultural value may perceive these students as using their time inefficiently.... [In addition], teachers should not assume that students who hesitate before answering a question in class do not have the correct answer or are unsure of the answer. Some students may need think time prior to responding to each question that is raised. Some cultures are more present- than future-oriented. This notion, which is particularly true for many Pacific Island cultures, promotes the attitude of seizing the day with less concern about tomorrow. Students, therefore, may need daily rather than long-term assignments. They may require direction and assistance in organizing and planning their time to complete long-term projects (1998, 32-33).

Huang provides other examples of the potential for cultural conflict related to time:

> Southeast Asians and Pacific Islanders [APIs] have a polychronic time (P-time) framework, in contrast to Western monochronic time. P-time allows different social interactions

to happen at the same time. M-time demands a linear scheduling of events. Teachers may be irritated when API parents come late for an appointment without an apology, or offended when APIs are inattentive to what they have to say. Because Asians perceive time as a simultaneous process, they are not aware of the linear scheduling of teachers' time. Similarly, some APIs, such as the Hmong, believe time per se can solve problems better than human intervention. They reason that one should not push hard in haste, but, rather, let events run their own course. An understanding of such a different notion of time may help teachers facilitate interaction among parents and staff (1993, online).

Social Structures as a Cultural Variable

Each culture has unique ways of organizing people to participate in learning events. Mainstream classroom structures may create confusion or disorientation for students from other cultures.

For example, many American classrooms emphasize individualism through learning tasks structured to feature independent work, competition, and "winning" as desirable pursuits. Such activities, however, may cause learning conflicts for some students of Central American or Mexican descent, because their cultures and home environments stress cooperation, collegiality, and group unity as important social behaviors. Consequently, competitive lesson structures may produce limited success with these students, while cooperative problem-solving or peer-oriented approaches may increase these students' engagement and achievement.

Sileo and Prather talk about the cultural characteristics of competition versus cooperation:

> Traditionally, individuals from certain Asian countries, such as China and Japan. are raised in individualistic or competitive environments. Students from other cultures, such as Filipino Americans and Pacific Islanders, however, are raised to be cooperative and group-oriented.... In the Hawaiian culture, for example, cooperation and assisted performance are commonplace; siblings are routinely responsible for the care of younger children in the family.... Students who have been

Asian American Learning Styles

Although diversity among Asian American groups makes overall descriptions difficult, there are general cultural characteristics, values, and practices shared by most Asians, particularly East and Southeast Asians, that are different from the mainstream American culture.

In many East and Southeast Asian cultures, Confucian ideals, which include respect for elders, deferred gratification, and discipline, are a strong influence. Most Asian American parents teach their children to value educational achievement, respect authority, feel responsibility for relatives, and show self-control. Asian American parents tend to view school failure as a lack of will and address this problem by increasing parental restrictions. Asian American children tend to be more dependent, conforming, and willing to place family welfare over individual wishes than are other American children.

Teachers in Asian cultures are accorded a higher status than teachers in the United States. Asian American children may be confused by the informality between American teachers and students, and expect considerable structure and organization. Asian children tend to need reinforcement from teachers and work more efficiently in a well-structured, quiet environment.

Self-effacement is a trait traditionally valued in many Asian cultures. Asian children tend to wait to participate, unless otherwise requested by the teacher. Having attention drawn to oneself—for example, having one's name put on the board for misbehaving—can bring considerable distress. Many Asian children have been socialized to listen more than speak, to speak in a soft voice, and to be modest in dress and behavior. While a student may be told at school to challenge others' views, the same child may be told at home to be quiet and not challenge authority. To avoid such conflicts, teachers can organize classroom activities around naturalistic interactions that permit the child to take the lead and to build upon modeling (Adapted from Feng 1994, online).

raised in cultures that foster cooperative behaviors may need direction regarding the appropriateness of cooperation in school. They may be quick to share their belongings with peers, which could potentially extend to allowing others to copy their schoolwork or answers on examinations. These students may view themselves as helpful or generous and, therefore, not interpret their behavior as inappropriate or problematic within the school's culture (1998, 333).

Likewise, Swisher and Deyhle contend that a competitive classroom structure may pose problems for some Native American children, who tend to avoid individual competition in which one person tries to outperform his or her competitors. In fact:

In many Indian societies the humility of an individual is something to be respected and preserved.... What the literature suggests is that for Indian children from certain groups, public display of knowledge that is not in keeping with community or group norms may be an uncomfortable experience—one that often causes Indian children to withdraw and act out the prototype of the "silent Indian child" (1987, 353-354).

Cognitive Styles as a Cultural Variable

Learning styles or cognitive styles are another realm of potential culture conflict. Numerous researchers have suggested that cognitive styles (typical or preferred modes of perceiving and assimilating information) may have strong ties to students' cultural backgrounds. Some investigators studying African American, Mexican American, and Puerto Rican children have found these students likely to display field-dependent or synergistic cognitive styles—recognizing holistic patterns and needing the "total picture" to process information. Most mainstream classrooms, however, tend to reward students who display primarily field-independent or analytical styles—perceiving parts of an object or task as discrete from their background and functioning well without a larger context for reference (Banks 1988). Such cognitive style conflicts may be one reason that some African American, Hispanic, and Native American children experience school difficulties.

Incorporating students' stylistic preferences into instruction ultimately may improve classroom learning for these children. However, some researchers and educators also fear that over-generalization about culture and cognitive style could lead to discriminatory treatment of student differences or provide ready excuses for student failure (O'Neil 1990).

African American Learning Styles

A summary of the research suggests that African Americans are field-dependent (holistic) learners as contrasted to field-independent and tend to:

- respond to things in terms of the whole instead of isolated parts;

- prefer inferential reasoning as opposed to deductive or inductive;

- approximate space and numbers rather than adhere to exactness;

- focus on people rather than things;

- be more proficient in nonverbal than verbal communications;

- prefer learning characterized by variation and freedom of movement;

- prefer kinesthetic/active instructional activities;

- prefer evening rather than morning learning;

- choose social over nonsocial cues; and

- proceed from a top-down processing approach rather than a bottom-up approach (adapted from Irvine and York 2001, 490).

Despite this concern, educators continue to explore cognitive style differences as a source of cultural mismatch in classrooms. Advocates suggest that teachers minimize the potential for stylistic conflict by incorporating a variety of stylistic preferences into instruction. Pointing to the broad continuum of cognitive styles that are present in students from all cultural backgrounds, many educators caution that teaching methods tailored to only one specific style may overlook or shortchange a large percentage of learners in any classroom.

Students from some cultural and ethnic groups, especially African Americans, Latinos, Native Americans, and Native Hawaiians, find formal, passive learning environments disconcerting, "cold," and distracting, so much so that they have difficulty concentrating on academic tasks. Many mainstream school procedures are linear (i.e., they use *topic centering*) (e.g., in terms of how information is arranged and presented; expectations about student behavior, such as lining up to enter and exit the classroom, sitting in straight rows). But the cultural structures of many ethnic groups are circular. In learning situations, students from many cultural and ethnic groups prefer group arrangements; responding in ways that integrate the affective, cognitive, and psychomotor dimensions; *topic-chaining* in the organization and presentation of ideas; and an environment in which all dimensions—humans, objects, space, and emotional tone—interact. An active, cooperative, warm, and emotionally supportive environment is fundamental to their effective learning (Gay 2000, 14).

Verbal Communication as a Cultural Variable

The first step in working with cultural differences in verbal communication is to more explicitly recognize some of the characteristics of classroom culture and of the students in these classrooms and understand how they might be less than compatible. Gay provides an example that could be happening in any classroom, on any day:

Teacher talk is an essential element of successful teaching. Yet, the same kind of talk is not equally effective with all kinds of students. For example, some students from some ethnic groups respond very well to questions directed to them as individuals, to discourse prompts that challenge them to think about issues and explain their thought processes in detail, and to explicit praise about their individual accomplishments. Students from other ethnic groups find such exchanges with teachers unnerving, so much so that they may drop out of instructional interactions entirely. For the first type of students, explicit, individual-focused interactions with teachers facilitate learning; for the second group, this type of teacher talk inhibits learning. In most classroom discourse, teachers dominate verbal interactions and almost exclusively control approved verbal opportunities and student tasks (2000, 9).

Latino Learning Styles

The research characterizes Latino students as field-dependent and relational learners, indicating that these students tend to:

- prefer group learning situations;

- be sensitive to the opinions of others;

- remember faces and social words;

- be extrinsically motivated;

- learn by doing;

- prefer concrete representations to abstract ones; and

- prefer people to ideas (Adapted from Irvine and York 2001, 490).

Delpit characterizes these cultural patterns inherent in verbal communication as codes or rules. From her perspective:

> [M]embers of any culture transmit information implicitly to co-members; however, when implicit codes are attempted across cultures, communication frequently breaks down. Each cultural group is left saying, "Why don't those people say what they mean?" as well as "What's wrong with them, why don't they understand?" (1988, 283).

Pennington concurs with Delpit's assessment of the problem and speaks specifically about communication style mismatches between some African American students and their White teachers:

> The style of communication and interaction in the majority culture classroom is often somewhat foreign to African American students.... Even direct issues in instruction are often obscured by non-African American teachers' uncertainty of how to obtain the best work via directions—said teachers

often give suggestions rather than provide direct commands. Hence, the student believes he or she has more expressive freedom than what later grading consequences would indicate (Pennington 2000, 38).

Delpit provides some examples of possible mismatches of "ways of talking" that could easily occur within the school setting. In one example, she categorizes "Is this where this book belongs?" as a teacher's "veiled command" that might be misunderstood by a child who would normally have been told at home "Put the book away," and who thus thinks that he or she is being given a choice. The misunderstanding can lead to further problems because "those veiled commands are commands nonetheless, [and] if veiled commands are ignored, the child will be labeled a behavior problem" (1988, 289).

Studies of Native American students highlight another example of a potential mismatch in the norms of verbal communication. Navajo and Choctaw cultures, for instance, typically feature long wait-times between one speaker's comments and the next speaker's response. Subtle nonverbal cues are used to determine turn-taking and indicate attentiveness to the conversation taking place. Mainstream classroom routines, in contrast, often require children to be quick to "take the floor" and call attention to themselves in order to participate in discussions or demonstrate their knowledge (Philips 1983). This assertive norm can exclude many Native American students who are reluctant to behave in a fashion that is considered unnecessary or even arrogant in their own community.

Au provides a common sense orientation for the discussion about teacher-student communication. To sum it up:

> The specific strategies teachers use are not so important as *whether or not the strategies make good sense to the children* (1980, 204) [italics added].

Nonverbal Communication as a Cultural Variable

Differences in behavioral cues and nonverbal communication patterns can also cause conflict. All children and teachers, regardless of cultural background, experience universal feelings such as excitement, interest, frustration, satisfaction, or confusion in the classroom. Ways of expressing these feelings, however, vary widely from culture to culture, and a single action or behavior can have contrasting meanings when viewed from different cultural perspectives.

For example, eye aversion is practiced among all major groups of color in the United States as an expression of deference to authority. Consequently, many African American, Latino, Native American, and Asian American students will not look directly at teachers when they are talking, which teachers may mistakenly interpret as a sign that these students are not paying attention. Yet, they may be listening intently (Gay 2000).

Kleifgen documents this potential for misunderstanding due to nonverbal cues in her study of cross-cultural encounters between teachers and limited-English-proficient primary school students. Teachers in the study discovered that unspoken rules governing interactions in the students' native cultures were very different from the standards followed in the dominant culture. For example, one student teacher, in an effort to be friendly and communicate well with a Korean kindergartner, placed himself on the child's level by crouching on his knees and sitting close to the student. The child was uncomfortable with this close contact, in accordance with the Korean cultural custom of maintaining a "certain physical space between him and his teachers as a signal of respect" (Kleifgen 1988, 222).

The teacher in this example later realized that his own style of being "warm" and "helpful" could be misinterpreted in a way that interfered with successful communication and instruction. An experienced teacher produced more successful learning encounters when this child's cultural norms of physical proximity and interpersonal interaction were used as guidelines for teacher behavior.

Huang provides additional information on ways in which nonverbal communication can contribute to cultural conflict and misunderstandings:

> High-context communication does not require clear, explicit verbal articulation. It relies on presumptions shared by people, nonverbal signals (e.g., body movement), and the very situation in which the interaction occurs. Low-context communication, on the other hand, involves intensively elaborate expressions that do not need much situational interpretation. While it is doubtful that the communication norms of any society, or even individual, are totally high- or low-context, API [Asian Pacific Islander] cultures are more high contextual, and Anglo American society is more low contextual.
>
> Like other low-context cultures, APIs, particularly East Asian Americans, are typically polite and even submissive in social encounters, but

Native American Learning Styles

Many researchers have noted that Native American students tend to be field-dependent and:

- prefer visual, spatial, and perceptual information rather than verbal;

- learn privately rather than in public;

- use mental images to remember and understand words and concepts rather than word associations;

- watch and then do, rather than employ trial and error;

- learn experientially and in natural settings;

- have a generalist orientation, interested in people and things;

- value conciseness of speech, slightly varied intonation, and limited vocal range;

- prefer small-group work; and

- favor holistic presentations and visual representations (Adapted from Irvine and York 2001, 490-491).

when a dispute persists they may suddenly become very hostile without providing warning signals. This happens because of the unconscious cultural conflict between low-context and high-context cultures. APIs, used to their high-context communication and, thus, constantly "tuned" to the moods of the other conversants during interaction, expect the others to be similarly sensitive. Westerners, who only pay attention to what is explicitly said, however, often ignore nonverbal cues. In an attempt to reach closure, and hearing no verbal disagreement and not noticing the nonverbal Asians' hesitancy, American professionals may move quickly toward resolution of the matter at hand. Then, when the Asian Americans finally explode in anger because they can no longer tolerate the conflict and are upset that their nonverbal messages were not received, the Westerners are surprised (1993, online).

To Sum Up

While this brief overview of cultural characteristics is not intended to provide a quick diagnosis of possible cultural conflicts for any individual child, it does highlight the importance of teachers' knowledge of the possibilities. In the next chapter, suggestions will be provided for teachers who are attempting to make instruction culturally sensitive and more effective for all children.

Chapter Two:
What We Know about
Human Learning and
Effective Instruction

The appropriate place to start the discussion of culture and teaching is what we know about both learning and good teaching and then use that knowledge as the bedrock for designing effective student-teacher interaction. Using this knowledge as a context for the discussion can serve as a reminder of how important it is for teachers to understand the strengths, weaknesses, and needs of all of their students—and to design instruction around these. It also suggests that teachers using a variety of teaching approaches in their classrooms may already be incorporating many culturally compatible elements into their instruction.

Key Findings of the Research on Human Learning

In the last few decades, research on human learning has produced a wealth of new information. Many of the conclusions of this research are inconsistent, but that is the nature of our evolving understanding of human learning. When the cognitive researchers take the additional step of applying their findings to make suggestions for practice and instructional strategies, the resource for educators is even richer. Below are some of the key understandings of the way people learn that have gained wide acceptance, with suggestions for how these findings can inform the teaching and learning process.

The Brain Searches for Meaning

"Whatever else we are as human beings, we have an innate desire for meaning," says Parnell (1996, 50). Learners of all ages discover meaning by making connections. Recent cognitive research tells us that the need for developing connections is rooted in the basic functioning of the brain itself. In simplified terms, each brain cell receives messages from other cells and decides to pass each message along depending on the amount of electrical charge behind the message. When it finds little or no connection, the message may be discarded. Every time a person experiences something that "connects" with a previous experience, that experience tends to "stick," and something is learned (Parnell 1996). In the classroom, this means that teachers should:

◆ Build curricula around what students already know. If facts are presented as part of a larger picture and associated with past learning, the brain is more likely to remember them (Bruer 1997).

◆ Create meaning by linking information to real-life experience. When possible, connect information to other personal associations (Jensen 1996).

◆ Use meaning-making activities such as journal writing. For example, at the end of each lesson, students may write down what they learned, how the learning relates to what they already know, and how they can use this information in the future (Sousa 1998).

◆ Use stories, complex themes, and metaphors to link information and understanding.

The Brain is a Complex System

The brain is a system of thoughts, emotions, imagination, and physiology that constantly exchanges information with its environment. As a parallel processor, the brain is able to perform many functions simultaneously (Caine and Caine 1994). Information broken up into small chunks, with supplied answers at every turn, does not take advantage of such complexity (Nadis 1993). What are the implications for teaching and learning? Schools should:

◆ Immerse students in experiences that encourage complex thinking.

◆ Avoid imposing artificial time limits on learning. Schedules should reflect the actual time it takes a student to complete a task, while maintaining a sense of coherence (Caine and Caine 1995).

◆ Allow learning to follow its own course. Recognize that the brain does not always take logical steps down one path, but can go down hundreds of paths simultaneously. With varied experiences, students make connections and extract patterns, absorbing and retaining a great deal incidentally (Della Neve, Hart, and Thomas 1986).

There Are Many Ways to Be Intelligent

Intelligence is multifaceted, defying measurement on an IQ test. Howard Gardner originally identified seven basic types of intelligence—linguistic, musical, logical-mathematical, spatial, bodily-kinesthetic, interpersonal, and intrapersonal—but he and other researchers acknowledge that there are more (Black 1994). This understanding suggests that teachers should:

◆ Provide choices so that students can pursue individual interests using individual strengths.

◆ Promote self-directed learning, in which students ask researchable questions, identify varied resources, and initiate, implement, and bring closure to a learning activity. Regardless of the focus—studying the nesting habits of local birds or solving a mock crime—these projects draw on numerous intelligences (Campbell 1997).

Learning is an Emotional Activity

Emotions often serve as a link for retrieving information and enhancing long-term memory. If we recall an event from years ago, most often there is some emotion attached to it (McClanahan 1998). In general, how a person feels in a learning situation determines the amount of attention he or she devotes to it. Students need to have an emotional connection to their work, their peers, and their teachers (Sousa 1998). How can educators use this knowledge to improve instruction? Teachers should, for example:

◆ Create a comfortable, nonthreatening climate. Anything that students might interpret as punitive, critical, or threatening may adversely affect learning (Della Neve, Hart, and Thomas 1986).

◆ Engage students personally through the use of journals, discussion, sharing, and reflection. If there is a significant current event that may have personal meaning for the students, ask them to talk or write about it.

◆ Use theater and drama—ideal forums to engage the emotions.

Learning is a Social Activity

Learning is heavily influenced by the interaction of the individual with the larger social environment. Our minds respond to interaction with others, in part because these situations often engage emotions, as discussed earlier. What are the implications for the classroom? For example, teachers should:

- Create a classroom atmosphere in which students interact comfortably and see themselves as part of a learning community.

- Look for opportunities for students to work in small-group settings.

- Use peer tutoring.

Metacognitive Skills Enhance Learning

Effective learners do more than acquire knowledge of facts and concepts. They have an awareness of how they are learning and use it to monitor their own thought processes and to change their approach to fit the situation or activity (Bruer 1997). Some researchers argue that "teaching thinking skills, learning strategies, problem solving, and creativity can make a difference as fundamental as how the brain itself works" (Languis 1998, 46). Metacognition involves being aware of one's strengths and weaknesses as a learner. What are some of the implications for teaching? For example, teachers should:

- Recognize the importance of teaching students metacognitive strategies.

- Involve students in discussions of their learning process and problem-solving strategies. By listening to students think out loud, teachers can recognize what specific understanding a student is missing, and then help the student obtain it (Bruer 1997).

The above characteristics of what research tells us about learning, along with the accompanying implications for teaching, can provide some immediate suggestions for making classrooms more culturally compatible without even discussing culture. For example, understanding that learning is a social activity and sometimes providing opportunities for student-to-student interaction will provide a more culturally compatible environment for students whose family lives accentuate the importance of cooperation.

What We Know About Good Teaching

Research also provides us with a solid base of information about good teaching. Themes that emerge stress the importance of these areas across both grade levels and disciplines. They include: 1) effective classroom management; 2) active engagement of students, using a wide variety of teaching skills and techniques, including a focus on individual students' needs; and 3) efficient use of instructional time.

Effective Classroom Management

Wilson highlights the critical relationship between classroom management and instruction: "The job of a teacher is first and foremost to instruct, not to manage. Yet management and instruction are inherently interdependent—in order for the learning environment to be at its best, both elements must be present, and working side by side, all the time" (1996, 2).

Wang, Haertel, and Walberg analyzed a knowledge base representing 11,000 statistical findings connecting a variety of variables and student achievement in order to answer the question: What helps students learn? Twenty-eight categories of factors, classified into six broad types of influences, such as student aptitude, classroom instruction and climate, and school organization, were rated as to their relative positive impact on learning.

Of the 28 categories, classroom management ranked first, with a "score" of 64.8, just ahead of student metacognitive processes (63.0) and cognitive processes (61.3). In the researchers' view, "effective classroom management increases student engagement, decreases disruptive behaviors, and makes good use of instructional time" (1993/1994, 76). Their definition of effective classroom management included effective questioning/recitation strategies, learner accountability, smooth transitions, and teacher "with-it-ness."

This last skill—"with-it-ness"—was further detailed in a study conducted by Morrow et al. designed to answer the question "What is the nature of exemplary early literacy instruction?" They found that exemplary teachers:

> . . . were extremely aware of what was happening in their rooms. They were virtually always in a position where they could see everyone in the room...[they] seemed extremely attuned to intervening before a problem escalated in the

classroom. Like good parents, these teachers seemed to possess a sixth sense for when things became too noisy, or even too quiet, in an area of the classroom. The high level of with-it-ness was a prominent element of the exemplary teachers' classroom management style (1999, 470).

Morrow et al. described other characteristics of effective classroom management leading to high student achievement:

> Teachers were consistent in their management techniques, so children knew what was expected of them and consequently carried out work that needed to be done. The day flowed smoothly from one activity to another, and routines were regular. The activities were varied to keep the children engaged. Furthermore, the affective quality in the rooms was exemplary; teachers were warm and caring.... In such an atmosphere, children learned to respect the teacher and one another (1999, 474).

Numerous other studies have also identified aspects of good classroom management as strongly linked to higher levels of student learning. These aspects include the following:

◆ The classroom management system emphasizes curriculum-related activities and maintaining student engagement in those activities (Brophy undated, 10). The teacher does not view discipline as a separate issue or as a "set of controls." Faced with a problem, such teachers "find something the student is interested in, find something else the student can do, find something else the student can share." In other words, these teachers "view discipline primarily as a natural consequence of their ability to interest and involve learners" (Haberman 1995, 5-6).

◆ The teacher is consistently well prepared and follows predictable, although not rigid, patterns of behavior and activities. Students know what is expected of them (Wharton-McDonald, Pressley, and Hampston 1998).

◆ The teacher minimizes disruptive behavior by redirecting students in a positive way before the problem becomes overt (Wharton-McDonald, Pressley, and Hampston 1998).

High Levels of Student Engagement

Many studies have found that the degree to which students are actively engaged in learning has a strong impact on the levels of student achievement (see, for example, Center on English Learning and Achievement 2000; Haberman 1995). Rather than trying to know what to do *to* students, teachers must work *with* students to interpret and deepen their existing knowledge and enthusiasm for learning. From this viewpoint, motivationally effective teaching is culturally responsive teaching (Wlodkowski and Ginsberg 1995).

Characteristics of effective classrooms that research has identified as increasing student engagement include:

- ◆ A positive and caring learning climate, in which constructive student and teacher social interactions take place. In these classrooms, students and teachers share common interests and values and emphasize cooperative goals (Wang, Haertel, and Walberg 1993/94; Brophy n.d.).

- ◆ Effective presentation of material and questioning. Teachers can prepare students for learning by providing an initial structure to clarify intended outcomes and cue desired learning strategies. The teacher explains content clearly and develops information with emphasis on its structure and connections. Questions are planned to engage students in sustained discourse structured around powerful ideas (Brophy n.d.).

- ◆ Sufficient opportunities for students to practice and apply what they are learning and to receive improvement-oriented feedback (Brophy n.d.).

- ◆ Attention to individual students' learning needs. The teacher provides whatever assistance students need to enable them to engage in learning activities productively (Brophy n.d.). One way in which effective teachers accomplish this is through "coaching/scaffolding," in which the teacher supports/prompts/coaches the child, providing just as much assistance as the child needs to perform a task (Taylor, et al. 1999).

In a study of 26 high-achieving, high-poverty schools in Texas, researchers identified attention to individual students' needs as a common characteristic of successful classrooms:

◆ The focus on the academic success of every student was evident in the planning of individual teachers.... Teachers planned lessons with a focus on getting each and every student to succeed academically. Teachers were attuned to the special ways in which individual students learned best. They exploited this knowledge to create learning environments that allowed many students to attain challenging academic skills . . . [and] formative assessments were used widely by teachers to assist them in planning instruction (Lein, Johnson, and Ragland 1997, 4).

◆ Instruction in metacognitive skills that enable students to learn more effectively. In effective classrooms, the teacher models and instructs students in learning and self-regulation strategies (Brophy n.d.). This helps students work toward more independence as learners (Wharton-McDonald, Pressley, and Hampton 1998).

◆ Use of a variety of groupings for instruction. Students often benefit from working in pairs or small groups to construct understanding or help one another master skills (Brophy n.d.). The "most accomplished" teachers in a 1999 study by Taylor et al. were most likely to use small, ability-grouped reading instruction. In their schools, a collaborative model was used "in which the classroom teacher, a resource teacher, an ESL teacher, and/or a special education teacher came together simultaneously and enabled every child, most typically, to have two blocks of small group instruction" (1999, 44). The small groups, while ability based, were also flexible, with periodic assessments used to review the placement of individual children.

Efficient Use of Time

An important teacher skill that has been linked to high levels of student learning in some studies is the effective and efficient use of instructional time. Teachers make efficient use of time through the following strategies.

Quality and Pacing of Instruction. Brophy and Good, in their review of research focusing on teacher behavior and student achievement, state that "the most consistently replicated findings link achievement to the quantity and pacing of instruction" (1986, 360). Teacher-driven variables in this broad category include:

◆ Role definitions and expectations. Achievement is maximized when teachers emphasize academic instruction as a major part of their own role, expect their students to master the curriculum, and allocate most of the available time to curriculum-related activities.

◆ Classroom management/student-engaged time. Engagement rates depend on the teacher's ability to organize and manage the classroom as an efficient learning environment where academic activities run smoothly, transitions are brief and orderly, and little time is spent getting organized or dealing with inattention or resistance.

◆ Consistent success/academic learning time. Students are engaged in activities that are appropriate in difficulty level and otherwise suited to their current achievement levels and needs.... Teachers must be effective in diagnosing and prescribing appropriate activities (Brophy and Good 1986, 360).

Curriculum Alignment. In classrooms that produce high levels of learning, "[a]ll components of the curriculum are aligned to create a cohesive program for accomplishing instructional purposes and goals" (Brophy n.d., 13). In these classrooms, the teacher establishes and follows through on expectations for learning outcomes (Brophy n.d.). Other research has pointed out that, in order to align the curriculum, the teacher must be aware of the purpose of instruction and be able to express his or her goals (Wharton-McDonald, Pressley, and Hampston 1998).

Effective Use of Assessment. Assessment can be an important tool to guide instruction and thus make the best use of classroom time. In productive classrooms, teachers use a variety of formal and informal assessment methods to monitor progress toward learning goals (Brophy n.d.).

In his review of the literature of successful teaching for low-income students of color, Zeichner (1992) identifies several key elements:

◆ Belief that all students can succeed and communication of this belief to students. This is done through such approaches as creation of a personal bond between teacher and students and/or the assignment of an academically challenging curriculum.

◆ Scaffolding or bridging between the cultures of the home and school. This would include, for example, "explicit teaching of the codes and customs of the school" (1992, 12).

- ◆ Teacher knowledge about areas such as child and adolescent develop-ment, second-language acquisition, and ways in which culture shapes school performance. The teacher must also know how to apply this knowledge in an instructional setting.

- ◆ Teaching strategies that focus on meaning-making and content instead of a focus on decontextualized skills.

As with the research about how students learn, some links between what we know about effective teaching, in general, and teaching that includes attention to culture are readily apparent. For example, researchers at the Center for Research on Education, Diversity, and Excellence (CREDE) propose the following five standards for effective pedagogy as "critical for improving learning outcomes for all students, and especially those of diverse ethnic, cultural, linguistic, or economic backgrounds" (Doherty, Echevarria, Estrada, Goldenberg, Hilberg, Saunders, and Tharpe 2002, online). They include:

- ◆ *Joint Productive Activity* (teachers and students learning together), which they describe as "especially important when the teacher and the students are not of the same background" because it "helps create a common context of experience within the school itself" (CREDE 2002a, online). An indicator of joint productive activity is instruction by the teacher in how students should work in groups, move from one activity to another, etc.

- ◆ *Language Development* (developing language across the curriculum), which the CREDE researchers describe as a "metagoal" and important because "literacy is the most fundamental competency for school success.... [However] the ways of using language that prevail in school discourse, such as ways of asking and answering questions, challenging claims, and using representations, are frequently unfamiliar to English language learners and other students at risk of educational failure. However, their own culturally based ways of talking can be effectively linked to the language used for academic disciplines by building learning contexts that evoke and build upon language strengths." If this standard is being implemented in the classroom, the teacher, for example, "assists written and oral language development through modeling, eliciting, probing, restating, clarifying, questioning, praising, etc., in purposeful conversation and writing" and "interacts with students in ways that respect students' preferences for speaking that may be different from the teacher's, such as wait time, eye contact, turntaking, or spotlighting" (CREDE 2002b, online).

◆ *Contextualization* (making meaning through connecting school to children's lives), a key element of effective instruction because "schools typically teach rules, abstractions, and verbal descriptions, and they teach by means of rules, abstractions, and verbal descriptions. Schools need to assist at-risk students by providing experiences that show abstract concepts are drawn from and applied to the everyday world." A teacher who is putting this standard into practice "acquires knowledge of local norms and knowledge by talking to students, parents or family members, or community members, and by reading pertinent documents" and "assists students to connect and apply their learning to home and community" (CREDE 2002c, online).

◆ *Challenging Activities* that teach complex thinking and challenge students toward cognitive complexity. The CREDE researchers describe the standard this way:

> Students at risk of educational failure, particularly those of limited standard English proficiency, are often forgiven any academic challenges on the assumption that they are of limited ability, or they are forgiven any genuine assessment of progress because the assessment tools are inadequate. Thus, both standards and feedback are weakened, with the predictable result that achievement is impeded. While such policies may often be the result of benign motives, the effect is to deny many diverse students the basic requirements of progress—high academic standards and meaningful assessment that allows feedback and responsive assistance.

> There is a clear consensus among education research ers that students at risk of educational failure require instruction that is cognitively challenging; that is, instruction that requires thinking and analysis, not only rote, repetitive, detail-level drills. This does not mean ignoring phonics rules, or not memorizing the multiplication tables, but it does mean going beyond

that level of curriculum into the exploration of the deepest possible reaches of interesting and meaningful materials. There are many ways in which cognitive complexity has been introduced into the teaching of students at risk of educational failure. There is good reason to believe, for instance, that a bilingual curriculum itself provides cognitive challenges that make it superior to a monolingual approach.

Working with a cognitively challenging curriculum requires careful leveling of tasks, so that students are motivated to stretch. It does not mean drill-and-kill exercises, nor does it mean overwhelming challenges that discourage effort. Getting the correct balance and providing appropriate assistance is, for the teacher, a truly cognitively challenging task (CREDE 2002d, online).

Teacher behaviors in support of this standard would include, for example, assisting "students to accomplish more complex understanding by building from their previous success [and by giving] clear, direct feedback about how student performance compares with challenging standards" (CREDE 2002d, online)

◆ *Instructional Conversation* (engaging students through dialogue) with teachers that has a "clear goal that guides the conversation with students [and ensuring that] student talk occurs at higher rates than teacher talk." Specifically, in instructional conversation, "teachers who use it, like parents in natural teaching, assume that the student has something to say beyond the known answers in the head of the adult. The adult listens carefully, makes guesses about the intended meaning, and adjusts responses to assist the student's efforts—in other words, engages in conversation. Such conversation reveals the knowledge, skills, and values—the culture—of the learner, enabling the teacher to contextualize teaching to fit the learner's experience base" (CREDE 2002e, online).

Obviously, most effective educators will recognize the instructional strategies described above as simply indicators of good teaching—even though, as the CREDE researchers emphasize, they may be especially helpful to students from non-mainstream cultures. Koki also reminds us that some instructional strategies that he describes as "non-Western" are now underpinnings of approaches, such as experiential learning, that are rapidly gaining popularity in U.S. schools:

> Traditional Western approaches to teaching tend to focus on the incremental acquisition of skills and reward students for mastering principles and procedures apart from any meaningful context, using abstract generalizations. Most non-Western approaches, on the other hand, use activities from everyday life as a foundation for the concepts and skills students are expected to acquire.
>
> For example, for years, remedial programs centered on "drill and memorization" of words and procedures. How to spell a word was considered more important than using the word in a sentence. Now we know that children learn to spell more quickly when they know how to use the word and have had frequent encounters with the word in various ways. As a result, new approaches to teaching engage students in research projects on multidisciplinary topics of interest long before students can write a perfect report. Similarly, the notion of "apprenticeship" that is used in many career preparation activities provides a meaningful real-life context where students learn the complex skills and concepts needed to make them become effective workers (Koki n.d., 4).

Finally, Strong, Silver, and Perini are clear: the current focus on standards—the *what* that students should know—should not be viewed as limiting *how* the content must be taught:

> A common curriculum does not imply a common instructional method. Some students learn more visually; others require discussion; still others favor direct instruction or project work. Attempting to elevate any one instructional strategy above the others guarantees that students whose learning styles differ from the common delivery system will suffer. A child who needs an imaginative approach to learning, or one who learns through conversation and dialogue, will not acquire the learning he needs and will therefore appear more and more disabled because of the school's refusal to address that learning style (2002, 65).

Teaching Styles and Learner Preferences

Implicit in the two sections above on what we know about teaching and learning is the connection between them—a connection that can either support or suppress high student achievement.

In the past 20 years, both researchers and educators have been paying more attention to the wide variety of ways in which individual students most efficiently acquire knowledge (student learning styles or preferences). This research base, along with more general knowledge about how students learn, has relevance for a discussion of culturally sensitive instruction, because the development of various learning styles is influenced by the culture of the home (Delpit 1995, Ladson-Billings 1994, 2001).

Research suggests that certain ethnic groups, in general, demonstrate various learning style characteristics. For example, Latino students might prefer group learning situations, learn by doing, and are more likely to be extrinsically than internally motivated. Native American students might prefer to learn privately rather than in public, prefer small group work, learn experientially and in natural settings (Irvine and York, 2001). Many African American children prefer instructional practices that are characterized by greater levels of communalism (group learning featuring social interdependence and connectedness), movement, expressive and physical stimulation of Afrocultural themes (Boykin and Bailey 2000).

While most teachers realize that a key to creating a successful learning environment for all students is to tap into the prior knowledge that students bring to school (Henze and Hauser 1999), research also indicates that teachers can increase the level of engaged learning and the academic achievement of students from different ethnic groups by modifying instruction so that it draws upon the students' cultural strengths—these learning preferences (Banks 1999).

Irvine and York stress the need for teachers to make effective connections between the learning and teaching styles in their own classrooms:

> Teachers also must negotiate and construct their understanding of teaching by examining the intersection of contexts and culture as well as their own behaviors, talents, and preferences. The cultural context of teaching and learning reminds

teachers to be attentive not only to individual students' learning styles but to their own actions, instructional goals, methods, and materials as they relate to their students' cultural experiences and preferred learning environment. The learning-styles research reminds teachers to: (a) understand and appreciate students' personal cultural knowledge; and (b) use their students' prior knowledge and culture in teaching. This process calls for the construction and design of relevant cultural metaphors and images in an effort to bridge the gap between what the students know and appreciate and the new knowledge or concepts to be taught. This process requires finding pertinent cultural examples, applying, comparing, and contrasting them, and creating authentic discourse and authentic teacher questions that relate what is being taught to what the student knows.

Second, the learning-styles research documents the importance of affect in teaching culturally diverse students. Teaching is an act of social interaction, and the resultant classroom climate is related directly to the interpersonal relationship between student and teacher.

Third, learning-styles research is extremely helpful in that it rightly places the responsibility for student learning with teachers, instead of ascribing blame to students and their parents. It holds teachers responsible and accountable for designing instruction to meet students' individual learning needs by making them aware that all students are capable of learning, provided the learning environment attends to a variety of learning styles. In addition, learning-styles research alerts teachers to ways in which their unique teaching styles and pedagogical preferences may contribute to lack of achievement by certain students. It stresses the importance of increasing the number of instructional methods and amount of materials in the classroom (2001, 9).

However, Irvine and York also repeat a caution against stereotyping that was made earlier in this publication:

[R]esearch on learning styles using culturally diverse students fails to support the premise that members of a given cultural group always exhibit a distinctive style. Hence, the issue is not the identification of a style for a particular ethnic or gender group, but rather how instruction should be arranged to meet the instructional needs of culturally diverse students. Teachers who understand the preferred style of a student can use that knowledge to design and plan instruction and to encourage students to experiment with a wider repertoire of learning approaches. Clearly, learning-styles research is a useful beginning point in designing appropriate instruction for culturally diverse students, and not an end in itself. (2001, 2).

Embedding Research on Teaching and Learning in Subject Area Instruction

Much of what has been learned in the last 20 years about teaching and learning is already being incorporated into recent subject area-based efforts to more actively engage students in learning. And many of the strategies also contribute to making teaching culturally compatible for a broader spectrum of students.

For example, research shows that learners link new information with personal experience and pre-existing knowledge by elaborating on the new information in order to integrate it. Teachers across subject areas can capitalize on this knowledge. When students are asked to discuss and write about personal experiences—and to make explicit connections between these and new subject area content—their communication skills benefit while they learn content. In addition, this approach can build on the cultural strengths of students whose past experiences include storytelling by family members. Sharing time, or "show-and-tell," provides students with another opportunity to practice skills of elaboration, summarization, etc., while also providing the teacher time to assess oral skills (David and Capraro 2001).

In mathematics, the standards now stress that students need opportunities to build understanding of math concepts in addition to calculation skills. Research has found that, through work in cooperative settings, students are able to provide more elaborate explanations of the concepts studied and that their mathematical reasoning is enhanced. This learning is strengthened when the teacher asks comprehension questions and connection questions that can be addressed in small groups, in addition to a variety of questions regarding strategies, tactics, or principles (David and Capraro 2001). Croom (1997) relates that the use of cooperative learning strategies in math promotes self-esteem and motivation as well as achievement among female and minority students, groups that have typically been viewed as underachieving in math. Thus, a commonly-used strategy such as cooperative learning can be inherently culturally sensitive. Also in mathematics, opportunities for hands-on involvement with materials helps to support children whose cultures are based on a learning-by-doing approach (Hale 2001).

Chapter Three:
Culturally Sensitive Instruction

Although the previous chapter makes clear the importance of understanding some fundamentals about teaching and learning—and then incorporating what we know into the classroom—proponents of culturally sensitive instruction caution us to go further. Culturally sensitive instruction does not assume that students and parents must always adjust to the needs and expectations of the school and the dominant culture. The accommodations are sometimes in the other direction. Teachers can better support students in developing their academic skills when they are able to build bridges between the cultures of the home and school.

A good first step to understanding culturally sensitive instruction is to briefly review four important features that provide the basis of this instructional approach.

The first feature is its pro-student philosophy. All students are seen as having the inherent resources and ability to experience academic success. It becomes the school's responsibility to ensure that avoidable culture conflicts do not thwart that inherent potential for learning. The idea is to capitalize on each child's strengths, viewing cultural ways of learning as resources to be used rather than deficits to be remediated. In Ladsen-Billings' (1995) view, a key goal of culturally relevant teaching is to get students to "choose" academic success, something they are more likely to do after experiencing it.

The second feature of culturally sensitive teaching is its development from a basic premise: There is no single best teaching method that will effectively reach all students at all times. Effective teachers diversify their instruction in response to individual students' interests, personalities, and abilities. The development of culturally sensitive instruction is a natural extension of this adaptive process. Teachers are not required to radically alter their philosophies of education or instruction in culturally diverse classrooms, nor are teachers being asked to develop a new, separate instructional system. Instead, educators can choose and selectively emphasize techniques within their existing repertoire of teaching behaviors that complement the characteristics of their students.

A third key feature of culturally sensitive instruction is its adherence to the "principle of least change" (Jordan 1985, 112). This framework suggests that only the minimum number of changes necessary to produce desirable learning effects should be undertaken at any given time. Limited modifications are chosen from a set of carefully prepared and researched instructional alternatives. This principle of least change, found also in special education literature, uses the existing skills of both teachers and students as the source of growth. Such a framework helps to make change a clearly defined, focused, and manageable process. In other words, teachers do not need to duplicate the cultural environment of their students' homes. Rather, both teachers and students can strive for mutual accommodation, treating each other's culture with respect while working together towards academic excellence.

The fourth key characteristic of culturally sensitive instruction is its emphasis on the maintenance of high expectations and high academic standards for all children. The key to success in diverse classrooms becomes "modifying the *means* used to achieve learning outcomes, not changing the intended outcomes themselves. School personnel need to set the same high academic standards and expectations for . . . all students, and they need to hold the students strictly accountable for meeting those standards" (Gilbert and Gay 1985, 133). In this way, equity and excellence are simultaneously maintained by a teaching system that features a single, common goal of educational excellence along with an understanding and use of the diversified paths that students travel to achieve that goal.

While there is general agreement that instruction can be made more culturally sensitive, there is considerable debate about the best way for teachers to take individual and group differences into account. The theory behind culturally sensitive instruction can be appealing, but how can such an approach be applied and evaluated in practice?

While cultural compatibility primarily strives to accommodate students' existing cultural characteristics and strengths, it also recognizes the desirability of teaching students to function within mainstream instructional

Kamehameha Early Education Project (KEEP)

The most frequently cited example of culturally sensitive instruction is the Kamehameha Early Education Project (KEEP). Developed to increase the school success of low-achieving Native Hawaiian students, KEEP was one of the first in-depth documentations of the implementation and effects of culturally appropriate schooling. Since the program was established in 1971, the goal of the educator-anthropologist teams at KEEP was to "produce a school program compatible with the culture of Hawaiian children in ways that will make the program educationally effective" (Jordan 1985, 109). To achieve this goal, KEEP teachers modified their classroom routines and organization to "mesh with the children's culture in ways that ensure the generation of academically important behaviors" (Jordan 1985, 110).

KEEP efforts were based on the observation that cultural conflicts greatly contributed to the low achievement of students at the KEEP school. To pinpoint precisely which culture conflicts were important in classrooms, researchers made carefully detailed observations of learning taking place in both home and school contexts. They found that traditional Hawaiian homes were highly peer-oriented. Children learned chores, roles, and traditions in groups of family members or friends. One-to-one adult/child interactions seldom occurred in children's early learning experiences. The school environment, on the other hand, emphasized independent work and direct teacher-student relations. These differences produced a cultural discontinuity that made students and teachers uncomfortable and hindered the educational process (Vogt, Jordan, and Tharp 1987).

The KEEP school staff, in response, modified their teaching methods, classroom organization, behavior management, and motivation strategies to reflect a culturally congruent peer focus. Cooperative and teacher-independent work groups became the classroom norm. By building on a familiar mode of learning, teachers were able to capitalize on their students' existing productive behaviors. Discipline problems decreased and on-task behaviors increased as the classrooms changed to match students' cultural characteristics.

No attempt was made to completely replicate Hawaiian culture in KEEP classrooms. Instead, teachers operated according to the "principle of least change," enacting the minimum number of research-based modifications necessary to produce school improvements (Jordan 1985). This principle of program development emphasized the selective use of skills that teachers already possessed. Techniques of coordinating small group work and encouraging on-task behavior were targeted in staff development. Such an approach made instructional modification manageable by employing small changes and providing continual feedback and support to teachers from the cultural research team.

The KEEP project reported dramatic achievement gains after four years of implementation. Although this process-oriented approach could be used with various school populations, the KEEP study was conducted in a setting characterized by a *single* cultural group. Despite this limitation, KEEP has provided valuable evidence that modifying instruction to be culturally compatible can improve student learning. The methods used to gather cultural information, the process used to support staff changes, and the transformation of the KEEP classrooms have also helped researchers in the fields of education, anthropology, psychology, and linguistics to further understand some of the complex connections between culture and student learning.

One implementation concern centers on the need for culturally sensitive programs to be closely tailored to the needs and cultural characteristics of particular groups of children. Each student population, school, and community has its own unique cultural environment. Because of the variations among cultures, a program such as KEEP that is found to be successful in one setting may not be effective in another setting, especially one in which many cultures are represented.

patterns. Delpit, a strong advocate of teaching children about their own cultures, nevertheless stresses the obligation of the schools to teach mainstream skills. She states that: "To imply to children . . . that it doesn't matter how you talk or how you write is to ensure their ultimate failure" (Delpit 1988). Culturally sensitive instruction aims to facilitate the acquisition of skills that schools provide as a common core of learning in society and works to ensure that all students have the chance to learn those skills in the way best suited to their individual needs. Culturally sensitive instruction might therefore be viewed as a technique used to ensure, not undermine, equity for students.

Another concern has implications for children in general, regardless of their background. Simply put, a system that teaches solely to strengths that are already present, without also attempting to encourage new skills and ways of thinking, may leave low-achieving students even further behind. Although such concerns make the issue of how to implement culturally sensitive instruction more complex, guidance is available for teachers attempting to make modifications to their instructional program. Singer defines the question of what techniques to use as "one of balance and timing: when to take advantage of cultural congruence, when to teach mainstream communication skills" (1988, 18).

On a day-to-day basis, alternating classroom time between mainstream and culturally sensitive modes of teaching may facilitate skill acquisition most effectively. To assist those students who do not initially respond well to mainstream techniques, familiar or culturally specific instructional methods can be used to present new or difficult material. Mainstream methods can then be used to further develop concepts, reinforce learning, and assist with skill mastery. This system of alternation expands skill development for all classroom students as they learn to absorb and apply knowledge in a variety of different ways. It is also compatible with the notion that good teaching requires that the teacher be continuously—and almost seamlessly—adjusting instructional approaches to the needs of the students.

A related issue involves the need to focus on what is being taught at a specific time in the classroom. While proponents of culturally sensitive instruction agree that, for example, failing to teach children standard English will do them a disservice in the long run, both research and the practice of some teachers who have had success working with students outside the cultural mainstream point to the need to ensure that the teaching of standard English does not hinder the teaching of other content areas.

Teaching Heterogeneous Groups

Diversifying instruction and focusing extensively on individual learners cannot be considered a simple undertaking. Cultural adaptations are constrained by the same limitations that are encountered whenever efforts are made to adapt instruction to other student differences (such as ability, age, developmental readiness, or interests). How can teachers maintain their effectiveness while teaching to widely varying student needs in heterogeneous groups? Will accommodating differences erode schools' ability to provide an equal set of skills and knowledge to all youth?

There are no easy answers to such questions, but educators studying cultural sensitivity are strong in their views that culturally sensitive instruction, if carefully done, need not entail negative side effects. They explain that culturally sensitive instruction does not seek to encumber teachers with the complete reconstruction of their pedagogy; rather, instructional changes are kept "rather small, not particularly radical, and well within the capabilities of most teachers" (Singer 1988, 25). Since these changes are designed to enhance, not supplant, effective teaching, they can be integrated into existing systems of instruction and are unlikely to interfere with teacher effectiveness.

Fears of Separation and Inequity

Perhaps the most frequently and strongly voiced arguments against culturally sensitive instruction focus on the question of whether it is desirable to single out students' cultural characteristics for attention. The process of identifying and using cultural traits as a basis for instruction must certainly be treated with caution. Both researchers and theorists warn that undue emphasis on cultural differences can create negative stereotypes that harm students, compromise high learning expectations, and impede school success (Irvine 1990).

Villegas stresses that uniqueness of each community and the individual differences within groups make it impossible to develop general solutions for the schooling problems of minority children. But she concludes from the existing research:

> We have learned that all students bring cultural resources to the classroom. We have also gained a new understanding of classroom life. Specifically, we have come to realize that the classroom has a culture, and that teachers can manipulate this culture for the benefit of all students (Villegas 1991, 31).

Finally, even the most carefully researched and implemented system of culturally sensitive instruction can be rendered ineffective if the classroom climate is not functioning in a supportive fashion. Culturally sensitive instruction demands a bias-free environment in which teachers maintain high expectations for all children.

Chapter Four:
Culturally Sensitive
Classrooms

Every hour of every school day teachers must juggle the need to create a supportive environment for learning with the press for academic achievement and the challenge of pursuing multiple strands of work so that students at varying places in their learning move ahead and none are left behind (Darling-Hammond 1997). The number and diversity of students who populate contemporary classrooms means that teachers continuously face difficult decisions if students are to learn at high levels. Such decisions include how to group students for instruction, which teaching strategies to use, and how to connect students' prior knowledge with the new content (Yiping, Abrami, and Spence 2000; Wlodkowski and Ginsberg 1995).

Teachers will be able to ensure high levels of learning from more students in increasingly diverse classrooms by learning how to use cultural characteristics as strengths instead of barriers to learning. Ladson-Billings (1994) views the "hallmark of the culturally relevant notion of learning [as recognizing] that something that each student brings to the classroom. Students are not seen as empty vessels.... What they know is acknowledged, valued and incorporated in the classroom." Shade, Kelly, and Oberg (1998) agree. In their view, the belief that all students come to school equipped and prepared with basic experiences and fundamental knowledge is key to successfully teaching a diverse population of students.

Banks et al. (2001) consider teachers' knowledge of their students' culture and ethnicity as proving an important "framework for inquiry" as they plan instruction. Culturally responsive teachers specifically acknowledge the presence of culturally diverse students and the need for these students to find relevant connections between their experiences and the subject matter (Montgomery 2001).

When teachers are challenged to use alternative instructional approaches with underachieving students of color, they commonly give one or both of the following responses: "Why lower standards for these students? Shouldn't all students be treated the same way?" or "Tell us what to do, and we will do it." The problem with the first response is that it reflects a significant misunderstanding about teaching ethnically and culturally diverse students. All too often, teachers equate using "alternative instructional approaches" with lowering expectations, which perpetuates the fallacy that treating all ethnically diverse students the same is a desirable way to teach. The problem with the second response is that no one can tell teachers *exactly* what to do with their *particular* students since effective teaching *is always specific* to the contextual and interactional dynamics of students and teachers in particular classrooms. The best that "outsiders" to these relationships can do is suggest possible directions to take and factors to consider as teachers seek out or develop alternative instructional strategies that might be more effective. But teachers must make the final choices for themselves (Gay 2000, 4).

When teachers and students share similar cultural and linguistic backgrounds, making connections is easier, because teachers have some fairly well-grounded information about the child's culture (Henze and Hauser 1999). However, all teachers should work to make effective connections. Nelson-Barber elaborates:

> The point is not that teachers need to share culture with students to be effective. Rather, teachers who are insiders to such knowledge can inform instruction and assist other teachers in learning how particular students learn best, how to organize schooling, how to discipline children, and so forth (1999, 5).

Trumbell, Rothstein-Fisch, and Greenfield report that teachers involved with the Bridging Cultures project have experienced success with their efforts to make instruction more culture-friendly:

> [They have] been amazed at how their increased awareness of culture—starting with their own—has enabled them to forestall conflicts in the classroom. They now recognize their own culture-based approaches to problem solving and can better anticipate their students' perspectives (2000, online).

In a culturally relevant classroom, instruction undergoes modifications to make it more congruent or compatible with the cultural and learning styles of minority students. Instruction—the way we teach—profoundly affects the way diverse students learn (i.e., perceive, receive, and retain the content of the curriculum). A culturally responsive teacher need not become an expert on every culture. Being culturally responsive does, however, require a basic understanding of some of the general beliefs, values, traditions, and norms that diverse groups hold (Ford and Frazier-Trotman 2001).

Sileo and Prater (1998) suggest that teachers begin by learning more about their students. For example, "What roles do silence, questions, and responses play in the students' cultures?" (See the box on page 56 for an extensive list of similar questions.) However, Irvine and York suggest that teachers also keep some critical questions in mind in an effort to refrain from making overly broad generalizations about culture and learning. For example, they could ask:

- Is culture the primary variable that influences learning styles of students of color? Are there other significant variables?

- Do characteristics of the cultural group apply uniformly to individual members of the group?

- What is the relationship between teachers' instructional methods and students' learning style?

- Should students of color always be taught using their preferred learning style? (2001, 492)

Taking the Next Step

Once possible cultural conflicts are identified, the challenge for teachers and other educators is to modify instruction so that learning can take place in the most effective way possible.

Gay talks about often difficult next steps for teachers. In her view, they:

> must do more than be "aware" or "tolerant" of cultural and linguistic differences. They must *do* something about their teaching processes. That "something" should involve using students' cultures, experiences, and orientations as instruc-

Questions to Identify Cultural Practices that Influence Students' Behaviors

Family Dynamics

◆ What are the important family rules?

◆ What are the primary disciplinary methods used at home and the students' reactions to these methods?

◆ Is the student praised, corrected, or criticized? How often and by whom?

◆ What are the behavioral expectations for children toward elders and teachers?

◆ What emotions are expressed openly? What emotions are never expressed?

◆ What messages are communicated to children nonverbally?

◆ Are shame and guilt used as disciplinary techniques?

Perceptions about Student Behavior

◆ What roles do silence, questions, and responses play in the student's culture?

◆ How do students' quiet and obedient behaviors (e.g., lack of overt responding and calling attention to oneself) affect the teachers' perceptions?

◆ Do students' inappropriate behaviors result from a lack of language proficiency and/or misunderstanding?

◆ Does the teaching style (e.g., teacher-directed instruction) differ from the student's accustomed learning style (e.g., peer-mediated instruction)?

Student Characteristics

◆ Do students question or obey authority figures?

◆ Do students assume a competitive or a cooperative posture in their learning and interaction with other students?

◆ Do students put their needs and desires before those of the group, or vice versa?

◆ What are the students' beliefs regarding sharing belongings with others? How do these beliefs affect classroom organization and expectations?

◆ Do boys and girls demonstrate differential behavioral expectations in their interactions with each other or with adults? Do students' perceptions about gender influence grouping patterns in the classroom or their interactions with and respect for authority figures?

◆ Do students maintain personal space or distance differentially in their interactions with other students of the same gender, opposite gender, or with adults?

Disciplinary Style

◆ What are acceptable and unacceptable ways to motivate or change students' behaviors, based on their perceptions of positive and negative consequences?

◆ What are acceptable ways to provide feedback to students about their academic and social behaviors?

◆ How do students' perceptions about group rights influence their willingness to change behaviors to benefit their peers? (Sileo and Prater 1998, 329).

tional tools for increasing students' achievement. In other words, much more teaching for ethnically diverse students should be filtered through students' own frames of reference than is currently the norm. In addition to being particularly useful for marginalized students of color, this approach benefits all students—an idea that is validated by general principles of learning. Experience has shown that "scaffolding" learning experiences, or creating opportunities for learning that build on previous experiences, enhances students' ability to master new knowledge and skills.... Before quality decisions can be made about the teaching practices that are most appropriate for ethnically diverse students, the aspects of teaching that are most problematic for these students must be identified. This can be accomplished by: (1) systematically analyzing the content and processes of teaching; (2) identifying conflict points between teaching and learning aspects of classroom content and instructional approaches that do not facilitate the learning of marginalized ethnically diverse students; and (3) making decisions about the kinds of changes needed to resolve these conflicts. This approach to improving instruction for diverse students is necessary because the mismatch between the way teachers teach and students learn often results in teaching and learning being much less effective. In other words, learning and teaching effectiveness are often the "causalities" of cultural conflicts in pluralistic classrooms (2000, 6-7).

Although teachers who are actively engaged in making their classrooms more culturally sensitive often find it difficult, they also typically find that the self reflection it promotes is valuable. One Bridging Cultures teacher reports:

I have a whole different perspective on culture and how it affects the decisions I make as a teacher. I see that my actions are culturally bound also (Trumbell, Rothstein-Fisch, and Greenfield 2000, online).

Pewewardy (1999) offers the following key principles to successfully guide teachers' efforts toward more culturally responsive teaching:

◆ Teachers use students' prior cultural knowledge as a foundation in the teaching and learning process.

- Classroom practices are compatible with students' language patterns, cognitive functioning, motivation, and the social norms and structures to which they are accustomed.

- Teachers value cultural knowledge, view students as assets, and integrate them into classroom instruction.

- Teachers act as cultural mediators and provide assistance through the use of questions, feedback, and scaffolding.

- Assessment practices and procedures reflect the diversity of student strengths and appreciation for multiple intelligences.

Embedded in Pewewardy's suggestions is the need for teachers to carefully study their own practices—practices that might have been successful with most of the students they taught in the past—and to think about them in terms of a more diverse classroom.

Gay provides an example of a teaching practice—the use of examples—that is used in most classrooms on a daily basis and reflects on how these can be used in more or less culturally responsive ways:

> A careful look at how teachers allocate time for speaking is revealing. Much of the actual act of teaching is devoted to providing examples, illustrations, vignettes, scenarios, and anecdotes to demonstrate the meanings and functions of concepts, ideas, facts, principles, and skills. The process begins with naming, defining, and explaining the idea being taught. All other subsequent instructional efforts are devoted to illustrating how, when, and in what situations, the idea or concept can be applied. These illustrations act as "bridges" between the abstract idea and the life experiences of learners. As such, they are the conduits or transmitters of meaningfulness in learning.... When teachers fail to use culturally relevant teaching examples, they inhibit the learning of students of color. This is not to say that students will never learn knowledge and skills that are not nested in their own frames of reference. Undoubtedly some will, but many will not, since abstractions are always more difficult to learn than practicalities.... An important way to make teaching and learning more effective for ethnically diverse students of color

is to broaden the pool of teaching examples so that they are culturally pluralistic. This requires teachers to understand the function of examples in teaching, to consider the types of examples they currently use, and to recognize the cultural limitations of these examples. They must then identify the types of examples that are best suited for different cultural groups; learn to create, locate, and/or solicit them; and decide how to incorporate them into regular teaching repertoires and routines (2000, 11).

Sileo and Prather believe that teachers should take a concrete approach to identifying and then adjusting for possible incongruities between teacher and student style. For example, teachers might use a three-column grid on which they:

> . . . write their personal cultural values, the comparative cultural values of the students with whom they are working, and strategies for developing sensitivity to any differences. For example, if the teacher's style is fast-paced and the student's style, on the other hand, is more slowly paced, with think-time needed when questions are raised, the teacher's strategy may be to allow the student the necessary time to think before offering a response to an inquiry (1998, 33).

This need not be a complex and time-consuming process. Gay suggests that teachers first focus on relatively simple changes that could be made to what she terms the "what" and "how" of instructional interactions. These could include:

- ◆ Extending wait time and changing turn-taking rules to honor the participation styles of students of different ethnic and cultural backgrounds.

- ◆ Using alternative cues to indicate attending behaviors, such as asking students to summarize points previously made, to restate another's point of view, or to declare their personal preferences on issues under discussion.

- ◆ Shortening the length of segments of teacher talk.

- ◆ Minimizing teacher talk by using learning strategies that are more student focused and active, such as small-group tasks, simulations, role playing, dramatic readings, and cooperative learning.

◆ Providing opportunities for students to establish, monitor, manage, and correct their own rules of classroom discourse.

◆ Honoring students' natural learning styles and ways of learning as much as possible. For example, teachers might encourage students to use cultural styles of storytelling to demonstrate their translation and reading comprehension skills, to present critical incidents in social studies, or to report the results of inquiry exercises or research topics. Teachers might also ask more divergent, higher-order cognitive and affective questions that give all students an opportunity to respond, and then accept students' affective reactions as legitimate contributions to the learning process (2000, 10).

Trumbell, Rothstein-Fisch, and Greenfield report that Bridging Cultures teachers have experimented with specific ways to make their classrooms more "culture-friendly" for those students with a more collectivist orientation and provide some simple changes that capitalize on children's values of helping and sharing:

◆ Select two classroom monitors rather than one, and allow them to work together.

◆ Allow students to help each other study vocabulary (students with greater English proficiency help those with lesser).

◆ Allow students to work in small groups to preview their homework assignments, discussing possible strategies for problems and assuring that all understand the assignment. (This also helps students whose parents may not be able to read the assignment in English.)

◆ Use choral reading, as well as individual reading.

◆ Have more than one "child of the week," so that the attention is shared.

◆ Share cleanup of the whole room at once, rather than having each group clean up an activity center before the children move to another (observed in a kindergarten classroom).

◆ Allow joint "ownership" of classroom crayons rather than a box per child (2000, online).

Debbie Diller, a White teacher, describes the changes in her teaching style as she began "using culture as a tool":

At the same time, I began to read voraciously the works of African American educators, such as Lisa Delpit, Madeline Cartwright, Violet Harris, and Gloria Ladson-Billings, to learn more. In my search, I came upon [Delpit's] notion of a teacher having a "high degree of personal power." I put this information into action and returned to my classroom a changed woman. The children didn't know what had happened. I began to give more explicit directives to students who were off task.

When Chris wasn't reading during silent reading time, I stood right beside him and said in a firm voice, "Chris, look at your book and read now." Before, I might have kneeled beside Chris and said in a quiet voice, "Chris, it's silent reading time. Would you please read your book now?" Chris responded to the more explicit approach, whereas he often ignored my indirect pleas. In fact, this worked with most of the challenging students in my class. The children had been telling me it was the best week they'd ever had at school and they didn't want to leave. The best way to describe this approach was summed up by Charlie at the end of my first week of using more personal power in my teaching style. As I walked them to the door, Charlie saluted me and said, "See you Monday, Sarge!" In retrospect, I think I was afraid of being authoritative with my African American students. When I held high expectations and commanded respect, both the children and I felt successful.

I found that most of my students learned best with the comfort and stability of a daily school routine with minimal changes or interruptions.... When my students knew what to expect, each day went more smoothly. When I told children exactly what they were expected to do and why, they were more successful. This worked for all my students, not just those who were African American.

At the same time, I began to use consistently the teaching style that Vickey [another teacher] had demonstrated to me—performer/audience style, a highly emotional interaction between Black performers and audiences, with a great deal of call and response. It captured the children's attention.... As I taught students a new concept, I encouraged them to respond chorally or individually at a rather fast, energized pace. "What sounds do you hear at the beginning of *stay?*" I'd ask enthusiastically. "st, *st*," the children would respond in rhythm. "Tell your neighbor another word that starts like *stay,*" I'd continue. "Tell your neighbor another word that starts with "st." The children would, spontaneously call out words to each other or to me. In the same way, when I read a story aloud, I let the children respond freely, "What's that word mean?" or "That reminds me of my Aunt Connie" in the middle of the story. I didn't insist on total silence. I read in *Black Children* [by Hale-Benson] that, in contrast, White audiences indicate attention by silence, eye contact, and laughter when appropriate. I had been trying unsuccessfully to get my young African American children's attention in a way inconsistent with their culture. When I spoke their language, they understood. So did I (1999, 823-824).

Valdez and Svedkauskaite, drawing from the work of Walter Secada, provide some other easy-to-implement suggestions. For example, "teachers can help support students by using behaviors similar to those used by mothers who are helping children learn to speak and converse." Specifically:

◆ *Simplify their speech.* In the classroom, teachers may use active voice and present tense, and provide objects, pictures, and manipulatives. Questions should be modified according to their linguistic complexity in a certain order: simple directives, yes/no, multiple choice, and wh- questions (who, what, when, where, why, which).

◆ *Expand their children's utterances in meaningful ways.* In the classroom, teachers should not comment on the linguistic construction but rather expand on what the student said by giving feedback

◆ *Scaffold their children's own language productions.* In the classroom, teachers should try to accept student answers in any language, including answers that are of limited linguistic complexity, by providing missing words or asking questions and gradually requiring increasingly elaborated sentences.

◆ *Focus on understanding what the child is trying to say.* Accordingly, teachers should focus on the content of the response, expanding the original utterance in their own responses as the need arises (2002, online).

Foster's review of research on African American teachers identified characteristics and practices that could be helpful to other teachers. She found that they use an "authoritative style that integrates acceptance and involvement, firm control, and psychological autonomy [and] . . . deliberately structure classroom activities to link classroom content to the experiences of their students" (2001, 576). They focus on the whole child, and attend to growth of social and emotional, as well as academic, skills. They use familiar cultural patterns in their instruction. For example, they encourage students to work together in a cooperative, collective classroom and work to build a sense of community. They incorporate culturally compatible communication patterns in their teaching. For example, they are more likely than teachers in general to use metaphors, analogies, call and response, and rhythm. As an example, Ladson-Billings describes a teacher who "used the lyrics of rap songs as a way to teach the elements of poetry . . . [then] went on to more conventional poetry" (1995b, 476).

It is clear that culture plays an important role in teaching and learning. However, Delpit (1995) reminds us that the goal is not how teachers can create the perfect "culturally matched" learning situation for each ethnic group, but rather how to recognize when there is a problem for a particular child and then to devise an approach that eliminates the barrier to learning.

Chapter Five:
Keeping Culture in Mind when Working with Families

An extensive research base developed over many years has made it clear that meaningful family involvement is a powerful predictor of student success in school (Davies 1993). For example, Henderson and Berla, after a comprehensive review of the literature on family involvement, concluded that "the research has become overwhelmingly clear; parent involvement—and that means all kinds of parents—improves student achievement." Specifically, they say:

◆ Educators hold higher expectations of students whose parents collaborate with the teacher.

◆ In programs that are designed to involve parents in full partnerships, disadvantaged students' achievement not only improves, but also can reach levels that are standard for middle-class children.

◆ Schools that work well with families have higher teacher morale and higher ratings of teachers by parents.

◆ A school's practice in informing and involving parents is a stronger determinant of whether inner-city parents will be involved with their children's education than are parent education, family size, marital status, and student grade level (Pape 1998, 19).

◆ Three critical elements occur when teachers and parents communicate and share in learning and growing together: 1) they form a bond in which the child's well-being is more easily and effectively addressed; 2) they serve as a source of support and renewal for each other (Swick and Broadway 1997); and 3) they become more aware of the concerns and problems each of them deal with on a daily basis (Jared 1997).

Teachers learn more about the students in their classes and are better able to provide appropriate educational services for their students hen families are actively involved in schools. Ultimately, students become more ready and able to learn—and more likely to stay in school and benefit from high-quality learning experiences. These positive outcomes happen regardless of ethnic/racial background, socioeconomic status, or the parents' educational level.

Challenges to Family Involvement

The benefits of family involvement in education are easily recognized, but school-home and school-community relationships can be fraught with tensions and challenges. Although these challenges are made more complex when the culture of the families is very different from that represented in the schools, there are basic ones that must be addressed. Barriers to effective parental involvement include time, lack of understanding of the academic decision-making process, perceived lack of interest by teachers, a feeling of disconnection, lack of training, inability to speak the dominant language, and lack of success (Shymansky 2000).

Research also suggests that a parent's decision to become actively involved with the schools depends on several factors:

◆ *Personal perception of their role in education.* What does the parent view as necessary and permissible to do? When parents believe they should be involved in their children's education, they are more likely to become so. But some ethnic groups see instilling proper behavior and respect as the task of families and instilling knowledge as the task of schools. For this reason, it is vital to stress the important role parents can play in influencing their children. Stress that the school expects families to teach basic skills and reinforce classroom learning.

Some parents would like to assist at the school but find that work often interferes. The school staff needs to be sensitive about constraints on parental involvement and work with parents to develop alternatives. One easy way to do this is to be flexible about scheduling conferences and meetings. Another is to tailor what you ask them to do in support of school to their jobs and work schedules.

◆ *Sense of efficacy.* Do parents view themselves as able to help their children do better in school? Parents who have done poorly in school may feel that they have little to offer their children and may be self-conscious about revealing their own academic difficulties. A common phenomenon these days is the language-minority parent who may feel ineffectual because he or she cannot read English-language textbooks very well. Another is the case of parents who did not do well in school or who did not graduate themselves. These parents may find it hard to believe that there is anything they can do to help their children succeed in school.

These are very touchy situations that call for great sensitivity. One strategy is for teachers to de-emphasize the skill or knowledge aspects of these parents' involvement. Instead, focus on how they can contribute to their children's positive attitudes toward school. Share with these parents the importance of having high expectations for their children and communicating the value of school to them. Teachers can also provide concrete, explicit examples of ways parents can support their children's learning. And, where possible, the school can make literacy activities and/or GED classes available to those who want them.

◆ *Parents' feelings of "welcomeness."* Parents are more likely to participate when they feel that they are genuinely welcome at the school. Provide a variety of options for participation and let the parent choose. Learn as much as possible from families about their cultural experiences, values, and attitudes. Consider personally inviting parents. When teachers take the time to call or write a personal note to parents, they are more likely to accept the invitation.

The Additional Challenges of Culture

As our nation's schools become more culturally diverse, so does the need for educators able to understand and truly communicate with families of various backgrounds. Manning and Lee remind us that "Educating all children requires working with all parents, regardless of their cultural or linguistic backgrounds . . . [and that] teachers cannot assume that parents of culturally diverse backgrounds share similar mindsets about teaching and learning as majority culture parents" (2001, 160).

For example, since Indochinese parents do not actively participate in schools in their native land and instead leave the responsibility for school to teachers

Family Learning Is Especially Important for Families with Language Challenges

Randolph Elementary School in Arlington, Va., provides an example of using family learning events to meet the special challenge of involving immigrant families. The school's 600 students speak more than 22 different primary languages, and English is the second language for most of them. About 64 percent of the students are Latino, and about 80 percent are from non-English-speaking homes.

Four years ago, the school developed an evening program to promote school involvement of non-English-speaking parents. Called "Family Night School," this program is designed to make families of immigrant children entering school more comfortable with the school and to help them make learning an integral part of their family lives.

The Family Night School is offered in several sessions each year, each consisting of about five meetings. A typical session includes a community dinner, parent training in some aspect of school involvement or in helping children develop the skills they need in school, instruction for students in basic reading and math skills, and paired parent-child activities.

The program plays a positive role in building a partnership between the school and these parents, whom many would consider "hard to reach." Says a staff member, "Success is sensed from being there, working with the parents and students, and watching their comfort level with the school setting grow over time."

Source: Educational Research Service (2001). "Family night boosts immigrant students' success through active parent involvement." *ERS Successful School Practices* (Spring 2001), pp. 5-8.

who are highly honored, they typically do not get involved with the schools in the United States. And, in many cultures, it would be quite natural for members of the extended family, such as grandparents or aunts, to come to parent-teacher conferences (Manning and Lee 2001).

Educators must also be aware that words may have different meanings in other cultures, and that cultures often have differing values. Quiroz, Greenfield, and Altchech highlight the example of a Latina immigrant mother reflecting on a conference with her daughter's first-grade teacher:

> I couldn't understand what the teacher was trying to communicate when she commented on my daughter's performance. I particularly recall two confusing comments this teacher made: "Your daughter is very sociable" and "Your daughter is outstanding in...." My tendency as a Mexican mother was to feel very happy she was sociable; after all, that was what I was fostering. However, I did not know what to do about her being "outstanding." I had tried to show my daughter not to "show off," but it seemed that it was not working (1999, 68).

An example from Mathews describes another area of potential cultural conflict for teachers who expect parents to be actively involved in discussing and making suggestions about their child's education:

> When South Asian and Southeast Asian parents seek advice, they want the teacher to take the active role and give them explicit directions on how to solve problems related to their children. This is because they view teachers as experts and authorities and thus believe that teachers will have all the resources to guide them properly. They do not normally initiate conversation and they are comfortable with silence (2000, 104).

Differences in cultural norms can also affect efforts to involve parents in school activities and committees. For example, Trumbell, Rothstein-Fisch, and Greenfield remind us that "immigrants from more collectivistic backgrounds may value consensus over the U.S. cultural norm of one man, one vote" (2000, online). Educators working with groups of parents will be more successful when keeping culture in mind.

As has been stated previously, potential problems with culture extend beyond interaction with students and their families who have recently immigrated to the United States. For example, Doris Walker-Dalhouse and Derick Dalhouse, two African American parents, talk about their experiences and those of many of their African American colleagues:

> Conferences for minority parents . . . are often more stressful
> because of the negative views frequently expressed about their
> children. If they perform poorly on standardized tests, the
> children may be labeled less capable, without considering
> their classroom and other types of performances. Their
> behaviors tend to be seen as aggressive or antisocial instead of
> enthusiastic or contemplative. They are viewed as being
> hyperactive and domineering rather than eager and showing
> leadership skills. These views emanate from stereotypic beliefs
> that children from cultures other than the dominant one
> come to school with problems and it is the job of the school
> to identify and correct them (2001, 76).

Another problem experienced in some schools as they become more culturally diverse is the difficulty that parents from different cultures may have relating to each other (National Council of Jewish Women n.d.). This may also need to be explicitly addressed as schools work to develop a sense of community.

The Bridging Cultures Project, a partnership among education researchers at WestEd, University of California, Los Angeles (UCLA), California State University at Northridge, and seven elementary teachers from six public schools in Southern California, has developed a framework to help educators identify and then "bridge" the differences between the dominant culture of U.S. schools and other cultures. In the view of Trumbell, Rothstein-Fisch, and Greenfield, the teachers involved with the project:

> . . . are finding it a powerful tool for understanding how the
> expectations for a student at school may conflict with the
> values of a student's family; how everyday patterns of class-
> room interaction can work at cross-purposes to the behavioral
> norms children grow up with (2000, online).

Two contrasting value systems—individualism and collectivism—are used as focal points for the teachers' study of culture and of the potential for conflict among cultures that can have a negative impact student learning. These value systems also affect family-school efforts to communicate and collaborate. For example,

> In every study comparing American parents to those of other
> cultures, even in other industrialized nations, the goal U.S.
> parents overwhelmingly stress is making their children inde-

pendent—socially and economically.... Collectivist societies, however, point their children in a different direction. Many immigrant parents from traditional cultures, for example, see their children's primary role as contributing members of the family unit. Children are expected to understand and act on a strong sense of responsibility toward the group, the family, and the community. Self-worth and esteem are not defined chiefly in terms of individual achievement.... In sharp contrast, young people in individualistic societies are typically expected to make educational and occupational choices that develop their own potential—not necessarily with any consideration for how their success would benefit their families (Trumbell, Rothstein-Fisch, and Greenfield 2000, online)

In addition to identifying potential sources of conflict among the cultures of most U.S. classrooms and some of the other cultures represented in schools, the Bridging Cultures Project encourages teachers to develop alternative responses or strategies. Two examples developed by Trumbell, Rothstein-Fisch, and Greenfield (2000) are presented below:

Independence Versus Helpfulness

◆ Potential for Conflict: Teachers may highly value children's ability to work independently and to focus on getting their own work done. But parents from a collectivistic orientation tend to care more about how helpful and cooperative their child is in the classroom. Teachers are likely to promote other behaviors or school practices that foster children's increasing independence from their parents, while parents continue to promote interdependence. For instance, parents may help their children in ways teachers deem inappropriate (e.g., tying their shoes), because it seems to perpetuate dependence.

◆ Situation: In one school that has a large population of immigrant Latino students, many mothers were "causing a problem" with the federally funded school breakfast program by accompanying their children to school, bringing along younger siblings, and eating breakfast with their children. Some were helping to feed their school-age children. In the eyes of school officials, who were responsible for implementing the federal program, the mothers and siblings were eating food that "belonged" to the children enrolled in the school. In fact, a condition of receiving the federal grant was that breakfasts be provided only to the school children. But teachers and administrators were also greatly concerned that the mothers' behaviors were inhibiting the children's development of independence—a goal of the prevailing U.S. culture in schools. The school addressed the problem by posting signs saying no parents would be allowed in the cafeteria during breakfast. The mothers, who were behaving according to their values of sharing and family unity, had great difficulty understanding the school's perspective and mobilized a protest that caused quite an uproar.

◆ Strategy: The school might have headed off a conflict by explaining to the parents why they could not accompany their children to breakfast and by simultaneously looking for other opportunities to invite whole families to the school to share a meal or other experiences. In the example above of mothers helping their children to eat, the mothers are acting as role models for helpfulness, which their children try to emulate—by helping even when helping is not an assigned task. In the classroom, a teacher can recognize and accept children's need to help others. Instead of having one "room monitor" or one person to do each small classroom job, pairs or small groups may do it together. Parents, too, like to be asked to help solve classroom problems or respond to needs and will come up with culturally appropriate strategies if the teacher establishes a climate of acceptance.

Parents' Roles Versus Teachers' Roles

◆ Potential for Conflict: The educational maxim "parents are children's first teachers" guides the thinking of many educators. Letters are often sent home urging parents to work with their children on specific academic skills, explaining this necessary role for parents. Sometimes schools suggest how many hours parents should spend working with their children, where to have the child study, and what supplies to have on hand. Some immigrant parents may not consider this an appropriate role for themselves. Seeing the functions of teacher and parent as clearly distinct, they may believe that academic instruction should be restricted to school. Moreover, if they had limited educational opportunities in their homelands, they may not have the subject-matter skills to tutor their children or help with homework. They may believe that their primary responsibility is to socialize the child, not to teach academics.

◆ Situation: When parents don't follow school suggestions to work on specific academic skills with their children at home, teachers may infer that the parents do not value education. Some schools also offer parenting courses, presuming that parents need instruction on how to discipline their children or prepare them for schooling. Yet, suggestions about how to rear children may not be well received. Moreover, the kind of parenting that individualistic teachers seek to promote may be seen as undermining the collectivistic values of home. Parents may wish that teachers would use the parents' socializing strategies more to produce more respectful students.

◆ Strategy: One Bridging Cultures teacher has developed a volunteer program that encourages parents to come into the classroom at their convenience and help in a variety of capacities. Because her classroom is a combined K-2, even parents with a limited education can assist with many of the early academic tasks. Not only do the Latino immigrant parents help the children, but some also learn along with them. Classroom instruction reinforces parents' literacy skills, in particular. When parents read to children from books written at a higher level than children could read on their own, children's linguistic models are stretched, as are parents' own skills. The presence of parents also introduces norms of respect for adults; at the same time, parents get to see how the teacher manages group discussions and elicits involvement from the students. In this particular community, the fact that this teacher is Latina and speaks Spanish provides maximum opportunity for developing understanding between home and school. Through this kind of volunteer program, parents can see how the teacher's role takes shape in a U.S. classroom; and teachers can glimpse the roles parents are comfortable with vis-à-vis schooling (Trumbell, Rothstein-Fisch, and Greenfield 2000, online).

Trumbell, Rothstein-Fisch, and Greenfield stress the importance of taking care when ascribing meaning to the actions of parents from different cultures:

> Immigrant parents have often come to the United States with the express goal of improving their children's educational opportunities.... They may want to become more involved with their child's schooling, but they may not know just how to comply with the expectations schools have of them. A seeming lack of compliance may result from parents' own limited educational experiences or from direct conflicts between home and school values (2000, online).

The Montgomery County Public School District (Md.), in cooperation with such groups as the Parents' Council of the local chapter of
the NAACP, has developed a booklet titled *Aim High! What Parents of
African American Children Should Know About Challenging Learning
Opportunities*. The guide is intended to "help parents become partners
with the [schools] to ensure that their children:

♦ develop strong academic skills and confidence as learners;

♦ excel in challenging instruction at all grade levels; and

♦ have increased opportunities for college acceptance, success,
and financial aid.

Content includes suggestions for ways in which parents can support
their children's education, addresses "commonly asked questions,"
and discusses ways in which parents can help their children cope with
negative peer pressure that may discourage academic achievement.

How Teachers Can Make a Difference

In their study of high-performing schools that served primarily Mexican
American students, Scribner and Scribner found that staff members in these
schools made specific efforts to build on the cultural values of the families.
They understood that informal small talk and personal contact is important
to building the family-school connection.

Trumbell, Rothstein-Fisch, and Greenfield describe just how important this
personal communication can be to establishing accurate home-school communication. For example,

> . . . immigrants from Mexico and Central America may not
> provide experiences in the home that promote text-based
> literacy. They may read to their children but not ask the
> children to respond to text the way more individualistic
> parents do (e.g., answer questions about what happened
> when, guess what might happen next, express their thoughts
> about the story). Instead, the value of reading to children may
> be seen primarily as a way of building family unity or passing

on moral lessons.... Because of possible cultural differences, when teachers and parents are setting joint goals in a parent-teacher conference, the teacher should not assume that suggested literacy activities for the home will be carried out in the expected way. Instead, [teachers should] make a point of finding out what kinds of activities the parent is comfortable doing and then build on those. And if parents are asked to participate in their children's homework activities, teachers must offer them a range of ways to do so. Often, parents feel more comfortable calling upon older children, who have been through the American school system, as homework helpers (2000, online).

Educators must know who their partners are and what they believe, value, and expect from the school and district for productive communication to occur. This information may be collected in a number of ways—for example, through surveys, small groups, or phone as well as face-to-face conversations with individual parents. More important than the method used to collect information is the underlying attitude of school staff. Ask parents for their input—and then listen carefully to what they say. Obviously, teachers have many opportunities to listen to parents, but building-level and central-office administrators should also spend time listening to parents.

Because the two-way sharing of information is a vital component of home-school communication, school personnel should spend at least as much time and energy listening and responding to the messages that parents send as they do crafting their outgoing messages to parents. Active listening requires focus, concentration, and practice—and a commitment to act on the feedback received from parents. Active listeners are rewarded with a richer understanding of parents' needs and beliefs and a treasure trove of useful information about students.

Bridging Cultures' teachers have found that an important component of successful communication with parents is taking a partnership approach, speaking in terms of "how we can meet the needs of students" instead of "what you need to do with your child." While the teachers present themselves as partners with the parents, they recognize that the parents will tend to defer to them as the experts on education (Trumbell, Rothstein-Fisch, and Greenfield 2000).

Al-Hassan and Gardner (2002) discuss some of the special problems—and then suggest tactics—for working with immigrant parents. These include:

◆ *Language barriers or even illiteracy.* Suggested Tactics: "First, try to assess and understand the language needs of each immigrant family. Your first task is to ask parents if they are comfortable receiving communication in English. You can informally assess whether English is an appropriate language for communicating with a family by talking with family members and evaluating if the parents or other significant adults in the family can effectively receive and give clear information.... [If] you realize that there is frequent miscommunication in English, then you can change the language of communication" (52).

◆ *Lack of information.* Suggested Tactics: "Provide examples of student behavior, preferably on graphs or charts that are more easily understood. Deliver positive messages through nonverbal communication; sometimes it is the only direct communication between you and the parent. Do not assume that you have communicated effectively; verify it by having the parents communicate to you what they heard" (54).

◆ *Teacher's Unfamiliarity with Immigrant Parents' Culture.* Suggested Tactics: "Ask bilingual parents . . . about their experiences with the education system in their native country. Be sensitive to matters pertaining to nonverbal communication (e.g., eye contact, facial expression, gestures, proximity, touching, clothing) among diverse cultural groups. In some cultures, looking directly and making eye contact could mean respect, but in other cultures it could be interpreted as disrespectful. Be careful with physical proximity and touching. Cultural norms vary widely on the type and frequency of touching that occurs during friendly professional interactions" (55).

◆ *Differing Views Regarding Involvement in Schools.* Suggested Tactics: "Assist families in making contact with other immigrant parents (from their native country) whose children have been successful in school" (57).

Quiroz, Greenfield, and Altchech (1999) describe a teacher who used her knowledge about the culture of her students' Latino immigrant parents to design parent-teacher conferences in a "culturally compatible" format. Instead of meeting with parents individually and having the students "lead" the conferences, she met with small groups of parents to explain her expectations for the students, test results, report cards, and ways in which parents could support their children. Time was provided for the students to take their parents on a tour of the classroom and to discuss their portfolios. Although the children were involved, the way in which they participated was more acceptable to the parents whose cultural values had made them uncomfortable when the children instead of the teacher had been leaders of the conferences.

Finally, key to the successful implementation of any family/community school involvement program is the understanding that, "Home-school collaboration is an attitude, not an activity" (Christenson n.d., online). While opportunities for families and school staff to interact are important, even more important is the quality of the interactions between them.

Chapter Six:
In Summary

A primary focus for public education at the national, state, and local levels is on improving student achievement and closing the achievement gap—whether among students from different racial/ethnic groups or among students of different socioeconomic groups.

A challenging curriculum is a common thread in efforts to close the gap. And this seems to be working in many schools. William Darity, lead author of a North Carolina study on closing the achievement gap, reports, "What we find in cases where schools have broadened their reach is that the children respond when they are given a more challenging curriculum" (Simmons 2001, online). But it is also clear that simply raising the bar is not enough.

Obviously, school personnel have limited control over some of the variables, such as low family income, associated with low achievement. However, they can actively address a wide array of problems, one of which is the cultural disconnect experienced by some students in our classrooms (Cooper 2000). Gay agrees and states that "achievement in academic subjects and basic learning skills will increase when the impact of culture on learning is clearly understood and routinely incorporated into classroom instruction" (2000, 4).

Culturally responsive pedagogy is consistent with the very nature of good teaching. It assumes that teachers will address the needs of each student in the classroom—and use the knowledge base about culture and learning to support this effort. But how should this be accomplished?

Cultural congruence—the use of culturally sensitive instruction—is an "inherently moderate" approach to educational change (Singer 1988, 1) that aims to incorporate small modifications into classroom routines. It does not address broader issues such as problems of teacher quality in high-poverty schools, the shortage of minority teachers, uneven distribution of funds,

school and class size issues, seeming problems with disproportionate placement of students of color in gifted or special education, an increasing number
of students who speak little to no English, or schools that are increasingly
segregated by race. Some people place priority on these broader issues and
urge educators to question the lasting impact of an approach that does not
address the systemic barriers that minority students face in school and society.

But advocates of cultural congruence assert that to wait until all these broader
issues are addressed will ensure failure for many students. They urge teachers
to use culturally sensitive instruction as a more readily accessible and immediate source for improving achievement. Koki agrees and places the issue in a
broader context:

> Many children have different ways of knowing and learning,
> and they will learn best when the context of activities and
> topics matters to them. What we have learned from efforts to
> improve education for minority children is also relevant for
> education that cuts across racial and socioeconomic lines.
> Culturally responsive education—at a time when educators,
> researchers, parents, and policymakers are concerned about
> the public education system and the richly diverse population
> that it serves—indeed has applications that reach far beyond
> mainstream or minority communities to the education
> community at large (n.d., 4).

Two common themes are found in the literature reviewed in this publication.
One is that the many different ways of learning found in a culturally diverse
student population can be assets, not liabilities, when incorporated into a
well-conceived educational process. The second is that cultural diversity and
commonality need not be opposing concepts in the classroom. The two
concepts are complementary when classroom instruction is directed toward a
common goal of educational excellence and incorporates students' diversified
ways of learning to achieve that goal.

Attention to issues of culture and learning has powerful implications for the
fostering of academic engagement and achievement of diverse student populations. Research indicates that teachers who maintain high academic standards and expectations for all of their students, who view each child's
strengths and ways of learning as useful resources, and who use a variety of
effective instructional strategies can successfully improve student learning.
These important characteristics of effective teaching in general are also key

features of culturally sensitive instruction that effectively addresses a diversity of student cultures, background experiences, and learning preferences. Effective teaching and cultural sensitivity thus actively reinforce one another to maximize each student's learning.

Teachers cannot do this alone. Waxman and Padron (1999) point to the need for leadership at the central-office and building levels. In their view, teachers will need strong support from administrators and extensive staff development. Schoolwide support systems, home-school partnerships, and staff development will need to be developed in support of teacher efforts to become more culturally aware. The search for ways to incorporate cultural sensitivity into instruction should be viewed as a part of our schools' larger educational mission to be responsive to the unique needs and characteristics of each student in the classroom.

Diversity in our schools is both an opportunity and a challenge. The more we know about the implications of culture and learning, the more we can effect productive solutions to maximize academic achievement for diverse learners and prepare all students for a future in a global society.

References

Abi-Nader, J. (1991). Creating a Vision of the Future: Strategies for Motivating Minority Students. *Phi Delta Kappan, 72*(7), pp.546-49.

Al-Hassan S., & Gardner, R., III. (2002). Involving Immigrant Parents of Students with Disabilities in the Educational process. *Teaching Exceptional Children* (May/June 2002), pp. 52-58.

Au, K. H. (1980). Participation Structures in a Reading Lesson with Hawaiian Children: Analysis of a Culturally Appropriate Instructional Event. *Anthropology & Education Quarterly, XI*(2), pp. 91-115.

Banks, J. A. (1999). Multicultural Education in the New Century. *The School Administrator* (May 1999), pp. 8-10.

Banks, J. A. (1988). Ethnicity, Class, Cognitive, and Motivational Styles: Research and Teaching Implications. *Journal of Negro Education, 57*(4), pp. 452-66.

Banks, J. A., Cookson, P., Gay, G., Hawley, W. D., Irvine, J. J., Nieto, S., Schofield, J. W., & Stephan, W. G. (2001). *Diversity Within Unity: Essential Principles For Teaching and Learning In a Multicultural Society.* Seattle: Center for Multicultural Education, College of Education, University of Washington. Retrieved from http://www.educ.washington.edu/coetestwebsite/pdf/DiversityUnity.pdf

Black, S. (1994). Different Kinds of Smart. *The Executive Educator* (January 1994), pp. 24-27.

Bowers, C.A., & Flinders, D. J. (1991). *Culturally Responsive Teaching and Supervision: A Handbook for Staff Development.* New York, NY: Teachers College Press.

Boykin, A. W., & Bailey, C. T. (2000). The Role of Cultural Factors in School Relevant Cognitive Functioning. *Center for Research on the Education of Students Placed at Risk (CRESPAR) Report* (April 2000), pp. 1-47.

Brophy, J. Undated. *Teaching.* Geneva, Switzerland: International Academy of Education. Retrieved from www.ibe.unesco.org.

Brophy, J., and Good, T. L. (1986). Teacher Behavior and Student Achievement. In M.C. Wittrock (Ed.), *Handbook of Research on Teaching,* Third Edition. New York: Macmillan Publishing Company.

Bruer, J. T. (1997). A Science of Learning. *The American School Board Journal* (February 1997), pp. 24-27.

Caine, R. N., & Caine, G. (1994). *Making Connections: Teaching and the Human Brain.* Reading, MA: Addison-Wesley.

Caine, R. N., & Caine, G. (1995). Reinventing Schools Through Brain-Based Learning. *Educational Leadership* (April 1995), pp. 43-47.

Campbell, L. (1997). Variations on a Theme: How Teachers Interpret MI Theory. *Educational Leadership* (September 1997), pp. 14-19.

Center for Research on Education, Diversity, and Excellence (CREDE). 2002a. "Joint Productive Activity." Santa Cruz, CA: Author. Retrieved from www.crede.ucsc.edu/standards/1jpa.html.

Center for Research on Education, Diversity, and Excellence (CREDE). 2002b. "Language Development." Santa Cruz, CA: Author. Retrieved from http://crede.ucsc.edu/standards/2ld.shtml.

Center for Research on Education, Diversity, and Excellence (CREDE). 2002c. "Contextualization." Santa Cruz, CA: Author. Retrieved from http://crede.ucsc.edu/standards/3cont.shtml.

Center for Research on Education, Diversity, and Excellence (CREDE). 2002d. "Challenging Activities." Santa Cruz, CA: Author. Retrieved from http://crede.ucsc.edu/standards/4chal_act.shtml.

Center for Research on Education, Diversity, and Excellence (CREDE). 2002e. "Instructional Conversation." Santa Cruz, CA: Author. Retrieved from http://crede.ucsc.edu/standards/5inst_con.shtml.

Center on English Learning and Achievement. (2000). Engaging Students in Meaningful Conversations Leads to Higher Achievement. *Newsletter* (Winter 2000). Retrieved from http://cela.albany.edu/newsletter.htm.

Christenson, S.L. Undated. Home-school collaboration: Building effective parent-school partnerships. Retrieved from www.cyfc.umn.edu/Learn/home.html

Cooper, R. (2000). Urban School Reform from a Student-of-Color Perspective. *Urban Education, 34*(5), pp. 597-622.

Croom, L. (1997). Mathematics for All Students. In J. Trentacosta & M. J. Kenney (Eds.), *Multicultural and Gender Equity In the Mathematics Classroom.* National Council of Teachers of Mathematics: Reston, VA.

The National Academy of Sciences. (1994). *Cultural Diversity and Early Education: Report of a Workshop.* Washington, DC: Author.

Darling-Hammond, L. (1997). *The Right to Learn.* Jossey-Bass Publishers: San Francisco, CA.

David, H. L., & Capraro, R. M. (2001). Strategies for Teaching in Heterogeneous Environments While Building a Classroom Community. *Education. 122*(1), pp. 86.

Davies, D. (1993). How to Build Partnerships that Work. *Principal* (September 2000), pp. 32-34.

Della Neve, C., Hart, L. A., & Thomas, E. C.. (1986). Huge Learning Jumps Show Potency of Brain-Based Instruction. *Phi Delta Kappan* (October 1986), pp. 143-148.

Delpit, L. (1995). *Other People's Children.* New York: The New Press.

Delpit, L. D. (1988). The Silenced Dialogue: Power and Pedagogy in Educating Other People's Children. *Harvard Educational Review* (August 1988), pp. 280-298.

Doherty, R., Echevarria, J., Estrada, P., Goldenberg, C., Hilberg, R. S, Saunders, W. M., & Tharpe, R. G. (2002). *Research Evidence: Five Standards for Effective Pedagogy and Student Outcomes (Technical Report No. G1).* Santa Cruz, CA: Center for Research on Education, Diversity, and Excellence. Retrieved from www.crede.ucsc.edu/research/pdd/5stand_evidence.html

Diller, D. (1999). Opening the Dialogue: Using Culture as a Tool in Teaching Young African American Children. *The Reading Teacher* (May 1999), pp. 820-828.

Feng, J. (1994). Asian-American Children: What Teachers Should Know (ERIC Digest). Urbana, IL: ERIC Clearinghouse on Elementary and Early Childhood Education.

Ford, D. Y., & Trotman-Frazier, M. (2001). Teachers of Gifted Students: Suggested Multicultural Characteristics and Competencies. *Roeper Review, 23*(4), pp. 235-239.

Foster, Michele. (2001). African American Teachers and Culturally Relevant Pedagogy. In J. A Banks (Ed.), *Handbook of Research on Multicultural Education* (pp. 570-581). San Francisco, CA: Jossey-Bass.

Gay, G. (1981). Interactions In Culturally Pluralistic Classrooms. In J. A. Banks (Ed.) *Education in the 80's: Multiethnic Education* (pp. 42-53). Washington, DC: National Education Association.

Gay, G. (2000). Improving the Achievement of Marginalized Students of Color. *In Including At-Risk Students in Standards-Based Reform: A Report on McREL's Diversity Roundtable II.* Aurora, CO: Mid-continent Research for Education and Learning.

Gilbert. S. E., & Gay, G. (1985.) Improving the Success in School of Poor Black Children. *Phi Delta Kappan 67*(2), pp. 133-37.

Good, T. L. (1987). Two Decades of Research on Teacher Expectations: Findings and Future Directions. *Journal of Teacher Education* (July/August 1987), pp. 33-47.

Gottfredson, D. C. et al. (1995). Increasing Teacher Expectations for Student Achievement. *Journal of Educational Research* (January/February 1995), pp. 155-163.

Graybill, S. W. (1997). Questions of Race and Culture: How They Relate to the Classroom for African American Students. *The Clearing House* (July/August 1997), pp. 311-318.

Guild, P. (1994). The Culture/Learning style Connection. *Educational Leadership* (May 1994), pp. 16-21.

Haberman, M. (1995). *Star Teachers of Children in Poverty.* West Lafayette, IN: Kappa Delta Pi.

Hale, J. E. (2001). *Learning While Black.* Baltimore, MD: The Johns Hopkins University Press.

Hale, J. E. (1994). *Unbank the Fire—Visions for the Education of African American Children.* Baltimore, MD: The Johns Hopkins University Press.

Heath, S. B. (1982). What No Bedtime Story Means: Narrative Skills at Home and School. *Language in Society 11*(1), pp. 49-76.

Henry, S. L., & Pepper, F. C. (1990). Cognitive, Social, and Cultural Effects on Indian Learning Style: Classroom Implications. *The Journal* of *Educational Issues of Language Minority Students 7* (Special Issue), pp. 85-97.

Henze, R., & Hauser, M. (1999). *Personalizing Culture through Anthropological Perspectives.* Santa Cruz, CA: Center for Research on Education, Diversity & Excellence (CREDE). Retrieved from http://www.cal.org/credepubs/edpractice.

Hoff, D. J. (2000). Gap Widens Between Black and White Students on NAEP. *Education Week* (June 6, 2000), pp. 1, 3.

Hollins, E. R., & Oliver, E. I. (1999). *Pathways to Success in School—Culturally Responsive Teaching.* Rahway, NJ: Lawrence Erlbaum Associates, Publishers.

Holmes, N. C. (2001). Under 18 Population More Diverse: 2000 Census. *Leadership News* (March 15, 2001), pp. 1-4.

Huang, G. (1993). Beyond Culture: Communicating with Asian American Children and Families (*ERIC/CUE Digest*). New York: ERIC Clearinghouse on Urban Education.

Irvine, J. J. (1990). *Black Students and School Failure: Policies, Practices, and Prescriptions.* Westport, CT: Greenwood Press.

Irvine, J. J., & York, D. E. (2001). Learning Styles and Culturally Diverse Students: A Literature Review. In J. A. Banks (Ed.), *Handbook of Research on Multicultural Education* (pp. 484-497). San Francisco, CA: Jossey-Bass.

Jared, E. J. (1997). Preparing New Teachers to Effectively Communicate with Parents. *Journal of Instructional Psychology, 24*(3), pp. 176-182.

Jensen, E. (1996). *Brain-Based Learning.* Del Mar, CA: Turning Point Publishing.

Jordan, C. (1984). Cultural Compatibility and the Education of Hawaiian Children: Implications for Mainland Educators. *Educational Research Quarterly, 8*(4), pp. 59-71.

Jordan, C. (1985). Translating Culture: From Ethnographic Information to Educational Program. *Anthropology and Education Quarterly, 16*(2), pp. 105-23.

Kleifgen, J. (1988). Learning From Student Teachers' Cross-Cultural Communicative Failures. *Anthropology and Education Quarterly, 19*(3), pp. 218-34.

Koki, S. (Undated). *New Research on Learning Indicates Need for Cultural Awareness Among Educators.* PREL Briefing Paper." Honolulu, HI: Pacific Region Educational Laboratory.

Ladson-Billings, G. (1994). *The Dreamkeepers: Successful Teachers of African-American Children.* San Francisco, CA: Jossey-Bass Inc.

Ladson-Billings, G. (1994b). What We Can Learn From Multicultural Education Research. *Educational Leadership* (May 1994), pp. 22-26.

Ladson-Billings, G. (1995). But That's Just Good Teaching! The Case for Culturally Relevant Pedagogy. *Theory into Practice, 34*(3), pp. 159-165.

Ladson-Billings, G. (1995b). Toward a Theory of Culturally Relevant Pedagogy. *American Educational Research Journal 32*(3), pp. 465-491.

Ladson-Billings, G. (2001). *Crossing over to Canaan.* San Francisco: CA: Jossey-Bass Inc.

Landsman, J. G. (2001). *A White Teacher Talks About Race.* Lanham, MD: Scarecrow Press, Inc.

Languis, M. L. (1998). Using Knowledge of the Brain in Educational Practice. *NASSP Bulletin* (May 1998), pp. 38-47.

Lein, L., Johnson, J. F., & Ragland, M. 1997. *Successful Texas Schoolwide Programs: Research Study Results.* Austin, TX: The Charles A. Dana Center, The University of Texas at Austin.

Lumsden, L. (1997). Expectations for Students. Office of Educational Research and Development (*ERIC Digest*).

Manning, M. L., & Lee, G. (2001). Working with Parents—Cultural and Linguistic Considerations. *Kappa Delta Pi Record* (Summer 2001), pp. 160-163.

Marx, G. (2000). *An Overview of Ten Trends: Educating Children for a Profoundly Different Future.* Arlington, VA: Educational Research Service.

Mathews, Rachel. (2000). Cultural Patterns of South Asia and Southeat Asian Americans. *Intervention in School and Clinic* (November 2000), pp. 101-104.

McClanahan, A. (1998). Brain Research Informing Classroom Practices. *Early Childhood.* Western Oregon University. Retrieved from http://www.tr.wou.edu/train/spring98/htm.

Montgomery, W. (2001). Creating Culturally Responsive, Inclusive Classrooms. *Teaching Exceptional Children, 33*(4), pp. 4-9.

Morrow, L. M., et al. (1999). Characteristics of Exemplary First-Grade Literacy Instruction. *The Reading Teacher* (February 1999), 462-476.

Nadis, S. (1993). Kid's Brainpower: Use It or Lose It. *Technology Review* (November/December 1993), pp. 19-20.

National Council of Jewish Women, Center for the Child. Undated. *Parents as School Partners: Research Project Overview.* Retrieved from http://Eric-web.tc.columbia.edu/families/NCJW_child/project.html

Nelson-Barber, S. (1999). A Better Education for Every Child: The Dilemma for Teachers of Culturally and Linguistically Diverse Students. Included in *Culturally and Linguistically Diverse Students in Standards-Based Reform: A Report on McREL's Diversity Roundtable I.* Aurora, CO: Mid-continent Research for Education and Learning.

Newsweek. (1999). Trying to Close the Achievement Gap. June 7, 1999, pp. 1-2.

O'Neil, J. (1990). Link Between Culture, Style Proves Divisive. *Educational Leadership 48*(2), pp. 8.

Pape, B. (1998). Reaching out to parents: Some helpful ideas for dealing with hard-to-reach parents. Virginia Journal of Education (December 1998), pp.18-19.

Parnell, D. (1996). Cerebral Context. *Vocational Education Journal* (March 1996), pp. 18-21.

Patton, J. M. (1998). The Disproportionate Representation of African Americans in Special Education: Looking Behind the Curtain for Understanding and Solutions. *Journal of Special Education. 32*(1), pp. 25-31.

Pennington, Harvey J. (2000). Issues in Mathematics Education with African American Students. *Multicultural Education* (Spring 2000), pp. 36-41.

Pewewardy, C. (1999). Culturally Responsive Teaching for American Indian Students. In E. R. Hollins and E. I. Oliver (Eds.), *Pathways to Success in School.* Rahway, NJ: Lawrence Erlbaum Associates, Inc.

Philips, S. U. (1983). *The Invisible Culture: Communication in Classroom and Community on the Warm Springs Indian Reservation.* New York, NY: Longman.

Quiroz, B., Greenfield, P.M., & Altchech, M. (1999). Bridging cultures with a parent-teacher conference. *Educational Leadership* (April 1999), pp. 68-70.

Saravia-Shore, M., & Garcia, E. (1995.) Diverse Teaching Strategies for Diverse Learners. In R. W. Cole (Ed.), *Educating Everybody's Children: Diverse Teaching Strategies for Diverse Learners* (pp. 47-74). Alexandria, VA: Association for Supervision and Curriculum Development.

Saville-Troike, M. (1978). *A Guide to Culture in the Classroom.* Arlington, VA. National Clearinghouse for Bilingual Education.

Schwartz, W. (2001). Closing the Achievement Gap: Principles for Improving the Educational Success of All Students. *ERIC Digest.* New York, NY: ERIC Clearinghouse on Urban Education. Retrieved from http://ericcass.uncg.edu/virtuallib/achievement/9021.html

Scribner, A. P., & Scribner, J. D. (2001). High-Performing Schools Serving Mexican-American Students: What They Can Teach Us. *ERIC Digest.* Charleston, WV: ERIC Clearinghouse on Rural Education and Small Schools. Retrieved from http://www.ael.org/eric/digests/edorc01-4.htm

Shade, B., Kelly, C., & Oberg, M. (1998). *Creating Culturally Responsive Classrooms.* Washington, D.C. American Psychological Association.

Sher, A., & Weast, J. (1991). Prizing Diversity: A Paradigm Shift In Schooling. *ERS Spectrum, 9*(2), pp. 7-12.

Shymansky, J. A. (2000). Empowering Families in Hands-On Science Programs. *School Science & Mathematics, 100*(1), pp. 48-56.

Sileo, T. W., & Prather, M. A. (1998). Creating Classroom Environments that Address the Linguistic and Cultural Backgrounds of Students with Disabilities: An Asian Pacific American Perspective. *Remedial and Special Education* (November/December 1998), pp. 323-337.

Simmons, T. (2001). Redefine talent, end racial gap, some say. *The News and Observer.* Retrieved from http://newsobserver.com/gap/story/1277520p-1310630c.html

Singer, E. A. (1988). *What Is Cultural Congruence and Why Are They Saying Such Terrible Things About It?* Occasional Paper Number 120, Michigan University Institute for Research on Teaching.

Sousa, D. A. (1998). Brain Research Can Help Principals Reform Secondary Schools. *NASSP Bulletin* (May 1998), pp. 21-28.

Steinberg, L., with Brown, B.B. and Dornbusch, S.M. (1996). Ethnicity and Adolescent Achievement. *American Educator* (Summer 1996), 28-48.

Strong, R. W., Silver, H. F., & Perini, M. J. (2002). *Teaching What Matters Most: Standards and Strategies for Raising Student Achievement.* Alexandria, VA: Association for Supervision and Curriculum Development.

Swick, K. J., and Broadway, F. 1997. Parental Efficacy and Successful Parent Involvement. *Journal of Instructional Psychology,* 24(1), 69-75.

Swisher, K., & Deyhle, D. (1987). Styles of Learning and Learning for Style: Educational Conflicts for American Indian/Alaskan Native Youth. *Journal of Multilingual and Multicultural Development,* 8(4), pp. 345-360.

Taylor, B., et al. (1999). *Beating the Odds in Teaching All Children to Read.* Ann Arbor, MI: Center for the Improvement of Early Reading Achievement.

Townsend, B. L. (2000). Standards-Based School Reform and Culturally Diverse Learners: Implications for Effective Leadership When the Stakes are Even Higher. Included in *Including Students in Standards-Based Reform: A Report on McREL's Diversity Roundtable III.* Aurora, CO: Mid-continent Research for Education and Learning.

Trumbell, E., Rothstein-Fisch, C., & Greenfield, P. M. (2000). *Bridging Cultures in Our Schools: New Approaches That Work* (WestEd Knowledge Brief). San Francisco, CA: WestEd. Retrieved from http://www.wested.org/online_pubs/bridging/welcome.shtml

Valdez, G., & Svedkauskaite, A. (2002). *Critical Issue: Mastering the Mosaic—Framing Impact Factors to Aid Limited English Proficient Students in Mathematics and Science.* Naperville, IL: North Central Regional educational Laboratory. Retrieved from http://www.ncrel.org/sdrs/areas/issues/content/cntareas/math/ma700.htm

Varney, S. S., & Cushner, K. (1990). Understanding Cultural Diversity Can Improve Intercultural Interactions. *NASSP Bulletin,* 74(528), pp. 89-94.

Viadero, D. (2000). Lags in Minority Achievement Defy Traditional Explanations. *Education Week* (March 22, 2000). Retrieved from http://www.edweek.org/ew/ewstory.cfm?slug=28causes.h19&keywords=achievement%20gap

Viadero, D. (1999). Gap Persists in Minority Achievement. *Education Week* (October 20, 1999), pp. 1, 11.

Viadero, D., & Johnston, R. C. (2000). Lifting Minority Achievement: Complex Answers. *Education Week* (April 5, 2000), pp. 1, 7.

Villegas, A. M. (1991). *Culturally Responsive Pedagogy for the 1990's and Beyond.* Princeton, NJ: Educational Testing Service.

Vogt. L. A., Jordan, C., & Tharp, R.G. (1987). Explaining School Failure, Producing School Success: Two Cases. *Anthropology and Education Quarterly, 18*(4), pp. 276-286.

Walker-Dalhouse, D., & Dalhouse, A. D. (2001). Parent-School Relations: Communicating More Effectively with African American Parents. *Young Children.* July 2001, pp. 76-80.

Wang, M. C., Haertel, G. D., and Walberg, H. J.. (1993/1994). What Helps Students Learn? *Educational Leadership* (December 1993/January 1994), 74-79.

Waxman, H. C., & Padron, Y. N. (1999). Teaching and Change in Urban Contexts. *Teaching and Change, 7*(1), pp. 3-16.

Weber, B. J., and Omotani, L. M. 1994. The Power of Believing. *The Executive Educator* (September 1994): 35-38.

Wharton-McDonald, R., Pressley, M., & Mistretta Hampton, J.. (1998). Literacy Instruction in Nine First-Grade Classrooms: Teacher Characteristics and Student Achievement. *The Elementary School Journal* (November 1998), 101-128.

Wilson, Elizabeth A. (1996). *What We Know About: Classroom Management to Encourage Motivation and Responsibility.* Arlington, VA: Educational Research Service.

Wlodkowski, R. J., & Ginsberg, M. B. A Framework for Culturally Responsive Teaching. *Educational Leadership* (September 1995), pp. 57-61.

Yiping, L., Abrami, P. C., & Spence, J. C. (2000). Effects of Within-Class Grouping on Student Achievement: An Exploratory Model. *Journal of Educational Research, 94*(2), pp. 101-113.

Zeichner, K. (1992). *Educating Teachers for Cultural Diversity ((NCRTL Special Report).* Lansing, MI: National Center for Research on Teacher Learning. Retrieved from ncrtl.msu.edu/http/sreports/sr293.pdf

Ziegahn, L. (2001). Considering Culture in the Selection of Teaching Approaches for Adults. *ERIC Digest.* Columbus, OH: ERIC Clearinghouse on Adult Career and Vocational Education. Retrieved from http://ericacve.org/docgen.asp?tbl=digests&ID=116

ORDER FORM FOR RELATED RESOURCES

Quantity	Item Number	Title	Base Price	ERS Individual Subscriber Discount Price	ERS Comprehensive Subscriber Discount Price	Total Price
				Price per Item		
	PRR-0491	*What We Know About: Culture and Learning*	$20.00	$15.00	$ 10.00	
Single copy only	PRR-5222	*Teaching Diverse Learners (ERS Info-File)*	$40.00	$30.00	$20.00	
Single copy only	PRR-5287	*Multicultural Education (ERS Info-File)*	$40.00	$30.00	$20.00	
Single copy only	PRR-5307	*Teaching English Language Learners (ERS Info-File)*	$40.00	$30.00	$20.00	
		Postage and Handling** (Add the greater of $3.50 or 10% of purchase price.)				
		Express Delivery** (Add $20 for second-business-day service.)				
	**Please double for international orders.				**TOTAL PRICE:**	

SATISFACTION GUARANTEED!
If you are not satisfied with an ERS resource, return it in its original condition within 30 days of receipt and we will give you a full refund.

Visit us online at www.ers.org for a complete listing of resources!

Method of payment:

☐ **Check enclosed**
    (payable to ERS)

☐ **P.O. enclosed.**
    (Purchase order #_____)

☐ **MasterCard**   ☐ **VISA**   ☐ **American Express**

Name on card: _____   Credit Card #:_____

Expiration Date: _____   Signature: _____

Ship to: (please print or type):

Name: _____   Position: _____

School District or Agency: _____   ERS Subscriber ID#: _____

Street Address: _____

City, State, Zip: _____

Telephone: _____   Fax: _____

Email: _____

Return completed order form to: Educational Research Service, Member Services Information Center
2000 Clarendon Boulevard, Arlington, VA 22201-2908
Phone: (800) 791-9308 • Fax: (800) 791-9309 • Email: msic@ers.org • Web site: www.ers.org

ERS SUBSCRIPTIONS AT A GLANCE

If you are looking for reliable K-12 research to...

... make the most effective education decisions, day in and day out

... make the most of the financial and human resources available to your school, district, or agency

... jumpstart your own professional development or inspire your staff and colleagues to do the same

... improve student achievement and ultimately make a difference in our children's future...

then you need look no further than an annual ERS Subscription!

- **Comprehensive School District Subscription.** All of the resources listed below are available in print free of charge or at a 50% discount to subscribing school district administrators, staff, and school board members. A copy of each newly-produced resource is shipped directly upon publication. (Annual fee based upon school district enrollment size.)
- **Individual Subscription.** The Individual Subscription is designed primarily for school administrators, staff, and school board members who want to receive a personal copy of new ERS studies, reports, and/or periodicals published. (Annual fee based upon school district enrollment size.)
- **Other Education Agency Subscription.** Subscriptions are also available for state associations, libraries, departments of education, service centers, and other organizations that need access to quality research and information resources and services throughout the year. (Contact ERS directly for annual fee.)
- **Eduportal Premium^R Subscription.** Gives entire administrative staff "instant" online, searchable access to the wide variety of ERS resources that until now were only available in print form. You'll gain access to the ERS electronic library of over 1,000 educational research-based documents from the last several years, as well as all new periodical content being gathered and analyzed. New content is constantly being added! (Annual fee based upon school district enrollment size.)
- **Eduportal Premium Plus^R Subscription.** All of the online resources described in the Premium^R Subscription above, PLUS a print copy of all new ERS periodicals and publications (mailed directly upon publication).

Research and information resources available through ERS subscriptions include:

- Two tiers of ERS information services:

  Info-Files—regularly updated collections of research and information on more than 100 education topics

  Custom Information Response—specially-prepared, customized information packet on any K-12 education topic you request

- *The Informed Educator Series*—ten concise research summaries on the hottest topics in American education
- *ERS Bulletin*—summaries of other education agencies' recently published research
- *ERS Spectrum*—quarterly journal of practical school research
- *ERS Focus On...*—quarterly all-in-one compilation of research, best practices, and related resources
- *On the Same Page*—brief research-based overview providing a balanced look at controversial K-12 issues
- ERS publications and related resources (videos, CD ROMs, and up to a dozen new studies and reports produced each year)
- Subscriber-friendly Member Services Information Center staff

ERS Subscription benefits begin as soon as your order is received and continue for 12 months. For more detailed subscription information and pricing, or to ask about any of the services or resources listed here, contact the Member Services Information Center toll-free at (800) 791-9308, by email at msic@ers.org, or visit us online at www.ers.org!

Notes

Notes

Notes

Notes

Notes

Notes

Notes